friends
with
jesus

by
Joseph Lange, OSFS
and
Anthony J. Cushing

VOLUME I
OF THE
LIVING CHRISTIAN COMMUNITY
SERIES

DOVE PUBLICATIONS
Pecos, New Mexico

PAULIST PRESS
New York, N.Y./Paramus, N.J.

Acknowledgements

Scripture quotations, unless otherwise noted, were taken from *The New American Bible*, with the permission of the Confraternity of Christian Doctrine.

Some quotations were taken from other versions:
Good News for Modern Man: The New Testament in Today's English Version, copyrighted by the American Bible Society, 1966 (indicated in the reference by TEV).

The Jerusalem Bible, Doubleday and Co., Garden City, N.Y., copyrighted by Darton, Longman and Todd, Ltd., and Doubleday and Co., Inc., 1966 (indicated in the reference by JB).

The Revised Standard Version, Ecumenical Edition, Collins, New York, 1973, copyrighted by the Division of Christian Education of the National Council of the Churches of Christ in the United States of America (indicated in the reference by RSV).

This volume, *Friendship with Jesus*, is the first of the four-volume *Living Christian Community* series. *Worshipping Community*, *Freedom and Healing*, and *Called To Service* will follow. Volume one was first published alone by Dove. This second printing of volume one and the remaining three volumes are co-published by Dove and Paulist.

Table of Contents

Introduction

After giving retreats and conferences over a good part of the United States, and after talking to hundreds and hundreds of leaders, it has become apparent to me that there is a clear need for more extensive teaching for those who are interested in drawing closer to God. Many of the people who are seeking this kind of new life have come to it through the Charismatic Renewal and have been exposed to hundreds of books, not all of which are good. There are, of course, many wonderful books from the spiritual masters of the past, but these are usually hard to get, and many of them do not deal with the kinds of problems that contemporary men and women have to face. Further, there are special problems which arise from involvement in a movement such as the Charismatic Renewal.

Over the past few years, a group of us in Allentown, Pennsylvania, have undergone a series of experiences that have led us to form a community, which we call the Children of Joy. The result of these experiences has been the development of a formation program consisting of instructions and pastoral care. We have experimented with different teaching materials and methods. What follows in this book and subsequent booklets is our teaching program as we have it now.

This book deals with the materials which are important as a foundation. The focus is on personal needs and personal choices, because we have found it is necessary to clear that up before other teaching can be heard. The other volumes cover material which is equally important, but necessarily put off until this first volume has been worked through. We do not say that this material is to be "mastered" or "understood," but rather to be "worked through." We are not at all interested in another intellectual achievement. The matter of these chapters is life with God. It is a matter of thought and prayer and personal choice. Subsequent volumes deal with freedom and healing and the communal dimensions of Christianity.

The experiences which are reflected in these teachings are the experiences which have changed our lives. What we talk about in these books is what has happened to us and to hundreds of thousands of others like ourselves. The reason for the following pages is our attempt to help others find what we have found, to experience what we have experienced. We have not expected enough from God and from our lives with God. We want everyone to know how good God is, how much He loves us, how good it is to share in His own Spirit, how abundant life is in the Church.

There are, then, four basic areas of experience which we are trying to communicate: (1) coming to know Jesus in a personal way, (2) experiencing the power of the Spirit, (3) growth in our relationship with God, and (4) growth with others in a community life. It is a basic conviction that we all have the Spirit of God from our baptism onward. A brief reflection on our childhood prayer and worship almost always reveals the fact of religious experiences in our lives, and that is the work of the Spirit. For a variety of reasons (e.g. the lack of example, the lack of teaching), few of us have reached the vision or the experience of a fuller life in Christ; so we have instead lived a kind of empty religious life, unaware of either God's promises or the joy of their fulfillment.

We are not speaking here of "experience" as a highly-charged emotional thing, any more than we would speak of the experience of marriage in that way. Rather we speak of what has happened and is happening to us. Sometimes it is joyful and sometimes painful. Sometimes it is exhilarating and sometimes barren. It is the stuff of human life illumined by a personal relationship with God through the power of the Holy Spirit.

We begin with a general description of our human condition and then contrast the world's answer and God's answer. Next we talk about God to remind ourselves that it is God with whom we deal, and not just someone else like ourselves. Then we speak of Jesus and how to get to know Him in a personal way. For Catholics we recommend the Sacrament of Reconciliation (or Penance) as the way to be reborn, to start over again.

Having come to know Jesus as Savior and Lord, we need to grow in that relationship, so we then talk about prayer. We have also found that it is important to learn the liberating and rewarding method of communicating love through prayer, so we teach and practice that next.

Then we talk about what we have learned about the Holy Spirit and about prayer in the Spirit. For all of us it opened up a whole new experience of God and of the presence of God among us. And as we lived with all this for a while, we began to encounter the problems of growth, the problems of continuity, the problems of commitment, etc. So we write about what is basic to growth.

We close with a chapter on the Second Coming, both because it is so rich and such an important theme of the teaching of Jesus and because it is so misunderstood.

Each chapter has a reading list of easily accessible books which are important in filling out what the chapter is about. We strongly recommend that they be read. We think of them as "required reading." The "suggested reading" is good supplementary reading, but not as important as the first list. Of course, there are hundreds of other good books not mentioned here, but we do not want to overwhelm the reader in the first few weeks! We have a lifetime to catch up on all the rest.

In order to get the most out of these volumes, we think it is extremely important to prepare for them by first entering into a spirit of prayer; by coming first before God and asking Him to give us faith and understanding. We should ask God to stir up the Spirit in our hearts so that we might hear what the Lord wants us to hear. We should read in a spirit of searching for the truth, the truth that can set us free, the truth that can bring us life, the truth that can help us find a new life with the fullness of God's love.

We suggest that it is a good idea to read each chapter through in its entirety and then go back and read it slowly. The second time through, try to carry on a conversation with the text. Underline, write in questions, jot down reactions in a notebook or in the margin.

For group use, we recommend taking a chapter a week with the recommended readings. The group leader can either point out the essentials of the chapter or let them emerge from discussion and then summarize with blackboard or newsprint. In any case, the essentials should be explicitly stated.

After the chapter on "Coming to Know Jesus in a Personal Way" we suggest that everyone spend the following week preparing for the Sacrament of Penance. Then, instead of going on to the next chapter, we have a communal penance service that session. It makes for an explicit choice, and it is important. This should be followed by some prayer time in which each one prays for healing from the effects of sin.

We have also found it valuable to teach about yielding to the Holy Spirit and the gift of tongues at the same time. The chapter tells why. Our experience has also been that it is good to take a week between this teaching and prayer for the release of the Spirit. Very often those in our program receive the gift of tongues and/or the release of the Spirit alone in prayer during that week. At the end of that week, after the discussion on charismatic prayer, we pray for all those who wish to be prayed with. We have also found that personal contact during that week is really valuable in helping people to deal with their difficulties.

Another thing we have found important is that we should not be bound to a schedule. If it takes two or three weeks to get through a chapter, or if it takes an extra session here or there to deal with difficulties, then take the time. We do not need to be rigid about covering a certain amount of material in a certain amount of time. What *is* important is that each one come to know Jesus and the power of His Spirit.

Finally, there are lots of ways of bringing people to a relationship with Jesus and the Father and the Holy Spirit. This way works for us and we share it with the prayer that it might be helpful to you.

May He be blessed in every way and may He come to be known and loved by all.

Joseph Lange, OSFS
Tony Cushing

by Joseph Lange

A General
Theological Perspective

It is discouraging and even frightening sometimes when you think of how little each of us realizes his potential. How much more we could be than we are! How many undiscovered painters, poets, sculptors, musicians, statesmen, athletes, architects! Even more discouraging is the thought of how few people really fulfill their potential to love themselves and others. How few people are really happy with themselves and their lives!

World history, too, is more or less a record of how men have mistreated each other, of how societies have attempted to work out schemes for bettering the lot of man, only to fall far short of that goal. And so there is poverty and racial or ethnic hatred, oppression, violence, war, greed — and so many other sicknesses, which have often enough been described by the ever-present prophets of doom.

Alongside the misery have been the glorious achievements of man, not the least of which has been the vision of what life *might* be, a vision usually accompanied by the feeling that this is what life *ought* to be. The vision is partially depicted by the various utopias, where men live in peace and love, creative and happy. But sadly, "utopia" today means "dream world." It has been the unrealizable dream of men; the real world just isn't like that.

This is where the Good News or Gospel fits in. What makes it both "Good" and "News" is that it says that *God* wants man to have more than he settles for and that He will give us the power to achieve it. To understand that more adequately and to

1

appreciate more deeply what the Gospel is about and why it has the power it does, it is helpful to begin by looking at ourselves.

OUR SEPARATENESS

Let each of these X's represent an individual human being:

X X X X X

Each one is distinct and separate from the others. Another way of saying it is that each of us is born in the flesh, encased in a skin, and by that very fact separated from all others. As our mental life develops, we begin to have an inwardness which is hidden from others. We learn to have our secret thoughts. We are trained to hide our feelings. One summer I was visiting some friends at the shore, and one of the children came into the room where we were. She looked at me for a moment and said, "You sure are losing your hair." I laughed, but the mother said, "We don't make comments about people's appearances." Of course, that is what we are all taught as we grow up: "Don't tell Grammom she's fat, the way you did last time." "Don't tell your cousin she's ugly."

The upshot is that very early in life we learn that people are not always what they appear to be. The clincher is the Santa Claus thing. Suddenly we discover that even our parents have lied to us. And all of this is a result of being human, of being born in the flesh, separate from others, with the capacity for a hidden inwardness.

As time goes by and we grow up some more, the effects of our not communicating with each other what we really think and really feel are a sense of isolation and aloneness — and there is no preventing this. Part of what it means to be human is this sense of isolation and aloneness. It is not so much a result of our choice as an effect of what we are: separate and capable of a secret inwardness. And all of this generates a fundamental insecurity and a fundamental fear. The insecurity comes from never being loved or accepted for what we really are, but only for what we appear to be. Deep down inside we know that people simply do not know us as we are; we just have not revealed all of our inwardness to them. The insecurity and sense of unworthiness is rooted in this radical non-communication. We

2

can always say to ourselves: "People compliment me and tell me how great I am and some of them even say that they love me; but if they really knew me, they wouldn't say that." As a result, many of the things that people say to us to make us feel good about ourselves and many of the things we say to others never hit the mark. We just don't feel they are totally truthful, and deep down we know that only the truth can set us free.

The fear that we live with, that we usually bury very deep, that can spring into our minds and hearts suddenly and without warning, the radical fear, is a complex thing. It is fear of rejection, fear of ridicule, fear of aloneness. The only remedy for it is to reveal ourselves totally to another and to find in him total acceptance. The risk involved is overwhelming, and hardly anyone cares to take it.

X X X X X

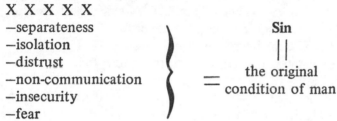

—separateness
—isolation
—distrust
—non-communication
—insecurity
—fear

Sin
||
= the original condition of man

SIN

Another word, the biblical word, for this fundamental description of what it is to be human is the word *sin*. It is the condition of each man simply because he is man: separate, isolated, with the capacity for secret inwardness. It is not something he is responsible for; it is not something he chooses; it is what he is. It really is very helpful, when you come across the word *sin*, to substitute words such as *isolation, non-communication*, etc. It helps because it translates *sin* into a word which connects more readily with our own experience, and it is our own experience of being human which we are talking about.

We do not feel guilty about our aloneness, but this original condition of each of us breeds the sins which do make us feel guilty. Because we do not really communicate with others, because of isolation and aloneness and insecurity and fear we do not love others as we might. We find it difficult and sometimes impossible to love. And so instead of love there is hatred, lying, deceit, anger, quarrels, cliques, prejudice, drunkenness, drugs, selfishness, distorted sexuality, murder, theft and all the rest. These are the sins which we commit because we are born into sin (i.e., into separateness).

THE WORLD

Now men have discovered and implemented ways of keeping themselves from each others' throats. They have invented laws, customs, and good manners to cover all the conceivable ways in which men interact with each other. *This is the way in which the world gives peace.* And this peace which the world gives is a real peace. It is the peace of good order, the peace which comes from knowing what to expect of yourself and of others. As long as the laws and customs and good manners are observed, there exists this peace which the world gives.

I think that it is also important to notice that the world defines goodness in terms of conformity to these laws, customs, and good manners. A man is good if he conforms, and the conformity is always *only* in terms of externals. The world does not worry about what is in a man's heart. It is enough that peace be maintained by external conformity to law and by being polite. So we have the superficial peace of the cocktail party, the office, the world. Change the style of your hair, no longer act as everyone else does, and the world condemns you as evil.

If you do not conform, you are required to reform yourself in order to be accepted. "I don't care what you feel. Shape up or get out." "I don't care whether you think it is phony or not. Do it." The reforming is always characterized by two things: (1) it concerns only external behavior, and (2) it is always achieved by one's own efforts. It breeds the pride of self-achievement. It's always shallow, but it has something noble and attractive about it.

I think it is also important to notice here that much of what passes for religion is quite simply this worldliness dressed up in religious language. It is just this kind of "religion" which has been justly condemned by Marx and Nietzsche and perceptive

4

people of all time. It is the result of man's almost irresistible penchant for externalizing everything, for reducing things of the heart to routines and roles. Then we have the letter, but not the spirit.

At any rate, we have this solution to the human condition as offered by the world:

The World's Peace

Peace $\begin{cases} \text{Laws} \\ \text{Customs} \\ \text{Good Manners} \end{cases}$ $\begin{cases} \text{Goodness} \\ \text{by} \\ \text{conforming and} \\ \text{reforming} \end{cases}$ $\begin{cases} \text{External} \\ \text{Superficial} \\ \text{By one's own effort} \end{cases}$

THE GOOD NEWS

On the other hand, we have the solution to the human condition which is presented in Scripture, that God formed a people and that from among them He raised the man Jesus as Savior and Lord. To understand what that means, it is helpful, I think, to begin with the message of some of the prophets of the Hebrew people.

Jeremiah said:

The days are coming, says the Lord, when I will make a new covenant with the house of Israel and the house of Judah . . . . I will place my law within them, and write it upon their hearts; I will be their God, and they shall be my people. (31:31, 33)

Ezechiel prophesied:

Thus the word of the Lord came to me:. . . . I will sprinkle clean water upon you to cleanse you from all your impurities, and from all your idols I will cleanse you. I will give you a new heart and place a new spirit within you, taking from your bodies your stony hearts and giving you natural hearts. I will put my spirit within you . . . . you shall be my people, and I will be your God. (36:16, 25-28)

And Joel, speaking the word of the Lord, said:

Then afterward I will pour out
  my spirit upon all mankind.
Your sons and daughters shall prophesy,

> your old men shall dream dreams,
> your young men shall see visions;
> Even upon the servants and the handmaids,
> in those days, I will pour out my spirit.

(3:1, 2)

The message of the Good News, of the new and eternal covenant, is that the Father has sent the Son and together They have sent the Spirit in order to change men's hearts. The New Covenant is the promise of God's new way of being with men. It is the promise that He will share His Spirit with all men in such a way as to save them from their isolation and redeem them from the superficiality of peace-by-conformity.

SALVATION

Salvation in Christ goes to the human heart and will not settle for less, will not settle for external conformity to law and good manners. Salvation in the New Covenant, in God's new way of being with men, promises to change our hearts of stone to hearts of flesh. Following Jesus and receiving His Spirit, rather than an empty external conformity to law, means that we will *want* to live for God, want to, from our hearts. There have been lots and lots of times that I have met people who have been afraid to accept the Christian message because they felt that it would require them to force themselves to give up things which they didn't want to give up. I would say to them: "Don't worry about it. If you accept Jesus, your heart will change. Your desires will change." As the Lord gave them faith to accept Jesus, this is exactly what happened to them, much to their amazement.

But, concretely, what does it mean to be saved? How do I experience "salvation"? In what way will my life be different because of the Gospel? What difference does it make to me that God has sent His Spirit? Go back for a moment to the description of the human condition, to each of us as isolated, alone, insecure, and fearful. What can save us from that? Victor Frankl says that anything which gives meaning to our lives will save us; and, in a sense, that is true. We can survive and even reach a measure of contentment by doing something which we consider to be worthwhile. There have been men and women who have devoted their lives to "doing their duty." Others have devoted their lives to music or science or art. The question of the Gospel, though, is not merely one of having life, but of having it more abundantly, of achieving the fullness of life.

Psychologists like Rogers, Buber, Sorokim, Laing, and Maslow speak of love as salvation: we find out who we are and appreciate ourselves and our uniqueness only be being loved for what we are. They speak of the liberating experience of love. And, of course, they are right. The remedy for the human condition, the original condition of each man, is to find freedom to be oneself with another, to be released from self-centeredness and from the dead-ends of the search for power or the search for security in possessions. To fall in love is to acquire a whole new perception of what is in the world and of what is of value. The whole experience of mankind attests to that. Infants have died because they have starved for love. Adults have committed suicide because of a lack of it. On the other hand, people have "come to life" because of love and have freely given all they have for it.

Still, no parents' love is fully adequate, and lovers are always insecure about their worthiness to be loved. The problem again is the human condition of isolation and a secret inwardness and the fear and distrust which it breeds. At a certain stage, children often stop communicating with their parents for fear of their disapproval. Lovers fear to reveal all of themselves to each other for fear of losing the love. Poor, fragile, human love seldom risks the ultimate. So many love relationships which began with so much promise end in disaster. What, then, is enduring salvation? What, then, is the answer? St. Paul puts it this way in Romans: "What a wretched man I am! Who can free me from this body under the power of death? All praise to God, through Jesus Christ our Lord!" (7:24-25)

The Good News is that the Father sent the Son and together They sent the Spirit so that we might know and experience Their love for each of us. Jesus told us that He is the Good Shepherd, that He knows us. To men who take that seriously, it can be terrifying. Paul Tillich says that the idea of a God who

7

knows us totally is one reason why some men hate God. In a way, it can be frightening to know that someone knows *everything* about us, our worst thoughts, feelings and actions included. Can you imagine someone who doesn't like you having that kind of information in his hands? But Jesus goes on to say that the Good Shepherd lays down his life for his sheep; that is, that He not only knows us as we have been and as we are now, but that He loves us just as we are, that He loved us even in our worst moments. I can remember saying that to a group once, and a girl exclaimed: "Wow! No one ever loved me that way before!" And, of course, she was right. No one can ever know us the way Jesus does, and so no one can ever love us as totally as He does. There is no way of hiding anything from Him, but we don't have to. He loves us as we are.

ACCEPTING HIS LOVE

Salvation in Christianity means accepting the personal knowing and loving of Jesus for me. Only in this acceptance of the love of the risen Jesus is my aloneness and isolation and insecurity fully conquered. So, to accept a love relationship with Jesus is to be saved from aloneness and the rest. That is why Jesus spoke of Himself as "The Way."

Notice, too, that Jesus does not require that we be good in a worldly sense or that we "reform" before He loves us. What the Good News promises, what makes it both "Good" and "News" is that by accepting His love we will be *transformed.* Love does that. When we choose to accept the love of another, our hearts are changed, our values change, our desires change — we are transformed. The difference between reformation and transformation is that reformation is a process of arduous self-discipline and self-achievement. Transformation is a burden that is easy, a yoke that is light, because it proceeds naturally from within the heart, a heart touched by love. The love of Jesus is experienced as a gift drawing us to a new life. Any love is experienced as a gift, but especially the love of an all-knowing Jesus.

So, we *experience* salvation by coming into a living

experience of the presence, power, and love of Jesus for us. He is the Way and his love transforms us.

But, Jesus is also the Truth. Face to face with Him, alone and before Him, we know the truth about Him, about ourselves, about material things, about the values of the world, about life and death. Imagine that Jesus appeared in your neighborhood and sent for each person there because He wanted to speak to each of you individually. Imagine that you were waiting with others outside of a room where He was. What would be your thoughts and feelings as you prepared yourself to face Him? Would you not see the truth? In fact, you can be alone with Him any time you choose, because He is always there.

And, further, Jesus is Life, because we are never more truly alive than when we are in love. And when the one who loves us knows us totally and loves us totally, then we not only have life, we have it most abundantly. I do not think we need to elaborate this point.

FREEDOM

Finally, concerning our salvation as individuals, the love of God for us sets us free — and that for two reasons. First of all, the love of another always releases us from our self-centeredness and all the limitations that go with it. As we become concerned about the other, our lives change in all kinds of ways. We experience a freedom from fears and the restraints of customs, and we experience a freedom to be ourselves with another person. The degree to which love liberates us depends on the depth of mutual knowing and loving. Again, only God's love and knowledge is total, so only His love sets us completely free. In John's Gospel Jesus says, "... if the Son frees you, you will really be free" (8:36).

Secondly, the love of God sets us free because He shares with us His Spirit. The very love and life which the Father and the Son share, they now share with all men who will accept it. To share in God's own Spirit is to be filled with His life and power. In another theological language we would say that by the grace (the gift of God's love, His Spirit) we live a supernatural life. Concretely, that means we share in the very power of God, the power to speak His word, the power to heal, to forgive, to know His will. Especially it means that we share in the power to know ourselves and others as He knows us and in the power to love ourselves and others as He loves us. It is a power we can trust in, a power released by our faith in it. It is an outstanding gift, something to meditate on and marvel at.

So, having been set free from fear and distrust, saved from our isolation and aloneness and insecurity, and empowered to know and love ourselves and others as God does, we can actually hope to achieve what men have always wanted: to live together in love. We can actually hope to fulfill the command of Jesus to love one another as He has loved us. We can hope for the realization of His prayer "that all may be one, as you, Father, are in me, and I in you" (John 17:21). To be as close to each other as Jesus is to the Father is awesome, almost unspeakable – yet we are promised the power in the Spirit to accomplish it. Praise be to Jesus, our Lord and Savior.

We can now expand our diagram to look like this:

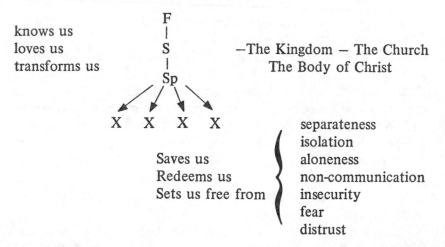

knows us
loves us
transforms us

F
|
S
|
Sp

–The Kingdom – The Church
The Body of Christ

X   X   X   X

Saves us
Redeems us
Sets us free from

{
separateness
isolation
aloneness
non-communication
insecurity
fear
distrust

COMMUNITY

And, with each man set free and empowered to love, we can more easily love each other. Thus we come to this next dimension of the new life in Jesus, the dimension of Christian community, the Kingdom of God, the Church. A follower of

Jesus is never saved by himself or for himself alone, but always with others and for others. Having accepted the saving love of Jesus, having been restored to friendship with the Father, having received the power of the Spirit, we are sent to build up the Kingdom, to begin to live with other Christians in a new community of love. No description of any aspect of our life in Christ is complete without this dimension of our living together in the Lord. This oneness Jesus said is to be the sign to the world that He was sent. "So shall the world know that you sent me, and that you loved them as you loved me" (John 17:23).

Again, how does it work? How do we experience this new life together in God? First, each one experiences the presence, the power, the love of the Lord for himself. And having been set free by that and empowered to love, each one is less defensive, less fearful, able to be vulnerable, more patient, more generous. So bonds of love begin to develop among us and we grow together in the Lord and in each other. Life in that community becomes characterized by these qualities which marked the early Christian communities: freedom in the Lord and with each other; the joy which comes from being right with God and oneself and one's neighbors; love; peace; and power.

I think that it is important here to notice that the peace which exists in the Christian community is radically different from the peace which the world offers. Jesus said: " 'Peace' is my farewell to you, my peace is my gift to you; I do not give it to you as the world gives peace" (John 14:27). The peace of the world comes from external, outward conformity. The peace of Jesus comes from being saved from emptiness and aloneness by knowing and loving Him and being totally known and loved; and the peace of Jesus is also the peace of living in a loving relationship with our brothers and sisters in our community. This is the promise of the new and eternal covenant.

THE POWER OF THE SPIRIT

It is also important to notice the power of the Spirit in Christian communities, for the Christian community is the Body of Christ, the continuation of the Messianic Presence, the redemptive presence. People coming into contact with this

11

community should experience the healing, forgiving, saving love of God. This Messianic Presence will have something of both the extraordinary and the everyday about it. There should be a sense of extraordinary faith, peace, joy, love and the other fruits of the Spirit. There should be signs and wonders accompanying the preaching of the Good News. There should be prophecy, tongues, the word of wisdom, the word of knowledge, and the other gifts of the Spirit. On the other hand, there will be the everydayness of people living together, making mistakes, forgiving one another, helping one another.

There will also be a sense of newness about the Christian community. There will seem to be a radical difference between life in the world and life in the community. The writers of the New Testament experienced this difference and tried to express it by such metaphors as "being reborn" and by the contrasts of "life in the Spirit" and "life in the flesh," "a life in darkness" and "life in the light." The newness is experienced as a newness of peace and joy and love, a newness in conversations, a newness in relationships, a newness in marriage, a newness in attitudes and behavior towards material things, a newness in the way people spend their time, a newness in creativity, in art and music and in all aspects of human life. This newness of life is the newness of the Kingdom of God, the fulfillment of the promises of Jesus.

Still the newness is both only a promise and a fulfillment in process. The Kingdom of God is a community of a pilgrim people, of a people already following Jesus, already saved from their isolation, already set free — but only partially. The final and total liberation comes only at the end, at Christ's second coming. Until then, the Kingdom is a Kingdom of the already and the not-yet. Already moving in the right direction, the journey is not yet complete. So the Kingdom is not made up of perfect people, but of people trusting in the power of the Spirit, confident that they can make the journey together, that they can work out their problems, that they can live in love. "In this way we are all to come to unity in our faith and in our knowledge of the Son of God, until we become the perfect Man, fully mature with the fullness of Christ himself" (Eph. 4:13–JB).

There is also present a newness of structure and authority and law in the community. The authority is from God and the organization is for good order. It is an authority of service in love and a willing submission to good order in love. Empty conformity to law in the Kingdom of God is not saving, but this is not the place to develop the idea more fully. Suffice it to say that law is not done away with in the Kingdom, but fulfilled in the Kingdom.

AN EXPERIENCE FOR TODAY

Finally, what we say about the Good News is not just a matter of more utopian ideas, but something we have experienced just as the apostles experienced it. It is happening now as it happened then. We can know Jesus and our Father and live with our brothers and sisters in the power of His Spirit. Christianity is not "religion" in the worldly sense of an external conformity to law, but a living relationship with God in our community. It is something to experience, as the apostles have said.

Peter wrote: "It was not by way of cleverly concocted myths that we taught you about the coming in power of our Lord Jesus Christ, for we were eyewitnesses of his sovereign majesty" (2 Pet. 1:16).

John wrote:

This is what we proclaim to you:
what was from the beginning,
what we have heard,
what we have seen with our eyes,
what we have looked upon
and our hands have touched——
we speak of the word of life.
(This life became visible;
we have seen and bear witness to it,
and we proclaim to you the eternal life
that was present to the Father
and became visible to us.)

13

What we have seen and heard
we proclaim in turn to you
so that you may share life with us.
This fellowship of ours is with the Father
and with his Son, Jesus Christ.

(1 John 1:1-3)

Paul wrote: "To him whose power now at work in us can do immeasurably more than we ask or imagine — to him be glory in the church and in Christ Jesus through all generations, world with end. Amen" (Ephesians 3:20, 21).

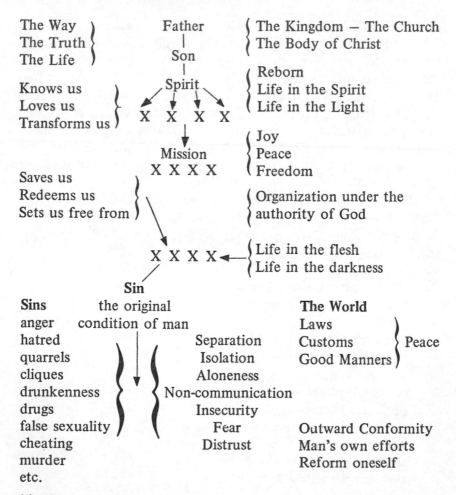

The Way ⎫
The Truth ⎬   Father   ⎰ The Kingdom — The Church
The Life ⎭ | ⎱ The Body of Christ
                        Son
                         | ⎰ Reborn
Knows us ⎫   Spirit   ⎨ Life in the Spirit
Loves us ⎬ ⎱ X X X X ↘   ⎰ Life in the Light
Transforms us ⎭

                         ↓   ⎰ Joy
                      Mission   ⎨ Peace
                      X X X X   ⎱ Freedom
Saves us ⎫
Redeems us ⎬   ⎰ Organization under the
Sets us free from ⎭   ⎱ authority of God

                    X X X X ◀——   ⎰ Life in the flesh
                     ╱   ⎱ Life in the darkness
              Sin
Sins   the original   **The World**
anger   condition of man   Laws   ⎫
hatred   Separation   Customs   ⎬ Peace
quarrels   Isolation   Good Manners ⎭
cliques   Aloneness
drunkenness   Non-communication
drugs   Insecurity
false sexuality   Fear   Outward Conformity
cheating   Distrust   Man's own efforts
murder   Reform oneself
etc.

BIBLIOGRAPHY

RECOMMENDED READING:

Martin, Ralph, *Unless the Lord Build the House,* Charismatic Renewal Books, Ave Maria Press, Notre Dame, Indiana, 1971, 63pp.
  This is a clear, insightful statement on the state of the Church today and the limitations of the various renewal movements within the Church. What is called for is a renewal of a personal, living relationship with Jesus.

Powell, John, *Why Am I Afraid to Tell You Who I Am?,* Argus Communications, Niles, Illinois, 1969, 167pp.
  Uses transactional analysis to identify, clarify, and overcome the barriers to authentic communication. The "how-to's" of interpersonal relationship.

SUPPLEMENTARY READING:

Haughton, Rosemary, *The Transformation of Man,* Paulist Press, New York, New York, 1967, 280pp.
  A study of conversion and community. A fantastic, in-depth, common sense treatment of the core of the Christian message. Excellent overview of the whole course — needs to be reread periodically.

by Joseph Lange

God

②

God is God. He is frightening and fascinating, mysterious and majestic, terrible and terrifying. In short, He is *holy*. This, I believe, is the most profound, the most important, and the most neglected revelation of the Bible. To describe it, let us begin with the words of Isaiah:

> ...I saw the Lord seated on a high and lofty throne, with the train of his garments filling the temple. Seraphim were stationed above; each of them had six wings: with two they veiled their faces, with two they veiled their feet, and with two they hovered aloft.
>
> "Holy, holy, holy is the Lord of hosts!" they cried one to the other. "All the earth is filled with his glory!" At the sound of that cry, the frame of the door shook and the house was filled with smoke.
>
> Then I said, "Woe is me, I am doomed! For I am a man of unclean lips, living among a people of unclean lips; yet my eyes have seen the King, the Lord of hosts!"
>
> (6:1-9)

The smoke or cloud that filled the temple had been a symbol of God's presence ever since the exodus (the journey of the Hebrew people from slavery in Egypt to freedom in the promised land). According to the description,

> The Lord preceded them, in the daytime by means of a column of cloud to show them the way, and at night by means of a column of fire to give them light. ... Neither the column of cloud by day nor the column of fire by night ever left its place in front of the people. (Ex. 13:21-22)

And while still on this same journey to the promised land, one day the Hebrew people camped at the foot of Mount Sinai and Moses went up the mountain to pray. While he was there, God told him to tell the people to prepare themselves for three days, for on the third day He would descend upon the mountain in the sight of them all. The mountain was to be roped off at the base and no creature, human or animal, was to approach beyond the ropes or he must be stoned to death. The description of that event goes like this:

> On the morning of the third day there were peals of thunder and lightning, and a heavy cloud over the mountain, and a very loud trumpet blast, so that all the people in the camp trembled. But Moses led the people out of the camp to meet God, and they stationed themselves at the foot of the mountain. Mount Sinai was all wrapped in smoke, for the Lord came down upon it in fire. The smoke rose from it as though from a furnace, and the whole mountain trembled violently. The trumpet blast grew louder and louder, while Moses was speaking and God answering him with thunder.
>
> When the Lord came down to the top of Mount Sinai, he summoned Moses to the top of the mountain, and Moses went up to him. (Ex. 19:16-20)

It was at this time that Moses received the ten commandments. He came down from the mountain, and the narrative continues:

> When the people witnessed the thunder and lightning, the trumpet blast and the mountain smoking, they all feared and trembled. So they took up a position much farther away and said to Moses, "You speak to us, and we will listen; but let not God speak to us, or we shall die." (Ex. 20:18-19)

So Moses took upon himself the task of meeting and speaking with the Lord. One day he said to Him: let me see Your glory. God answered:

> I will make all my beauty pass before you, and in your presence I will pronounce my name, "Lord"; I who show favors to whom I will, I who grant mercy to whom I will.

But my face you cannot see, for no man sees me and still lives." (Ex. 33:19-20)

It was also at this time that Moses received the directions for the making of the Ark of the Covenant and the tent that would cover it. Once this was made, the cloud that had accompanied the Israelites settled over the tent of the Ark. When Solomon's temple was finally finished and the Ark placed in the inner sanctuary, the cloud once again appeared, this time for the last time, and it filled the whole temple. And Solomon said: "The Lord intends to dwell in the dark cloud" (3 Kgs. 8:12).

THE HOLY GOD OF ISRAEL

I think that sums it up nicely. The cloud was a symbol of God's presence with His people; but at the same time it also symbolized the fact that God was unknowable, mysterious, hidden. Our vision cannot penetrate a cloud, and our minds cannot fathom the immensity or the mystery of God. The word *holy*, which the Seraphim used in the vision of Isaiah, originally had the same meaning: set apart, distinct from, above and beyond. This was the Hebrew notion of God from the very beginning, and the holy God of Israel was unique throughout all the ancient cultures for this very reason, as we mentioned above. The Hebrew God was holy. He was above and beyond the world; He existed before the world began— in fact, He created it.

The point of all this is that we do not know God as He really is, simply because we cannot. He is different from ourselves. He is not a man or even a superman, which is why He has been aptly described as "The Entirely Other." There is no doubt that we never really know another as well as we know ourselves. We can guess at his secret thoughts and motives because in many ways he is like us. Not so with God. He is the Entirely Other. Again in Isaiah we hear God speaking to us:

For my thoughts are not your thoughts,
nor are your ways my ways, says the Lord.
As high as the heavens are above the earth,
so high are my ways above your ways
and my thoughts above your thoughts.

(55:8, 9)

This idea of God, which we find revealed in the pages of Sacred Scripture, is that of a God so far above and beyond all creation that no created thing, man included, could bear to see Him. The experience would be more than we could endure. "To see God is to die" is a phrase that occurs again and again in the Old Testament. In the vision of Isaiah even the Seraphim covered their eyes so that they would not see Him! This is the aspect of holiness which arises from the majesty and mystery of the Entirely Other.

FEAR AND FASCINATION

We are all familiar with the feeling of uneasiness, of fear, which takes hold of us in the darkness of an unfamiliar deserted house. Ghost stories play upon those feelings, and they are often accompanied by "crawling of the flesh" or goose-pimples. We are afraid of the uncanny, of the mysterious. In an extreme situation it can be terrifying. It can also be fascinating and alluring. How many have felt almost irresistibly drawn to investigate a deserted house or a dark cavern, or just to walk through a cemetery at night alone? How many have been fascinated and drawn to flirtation with death? These too, are aspects of holiness; for that which is holy is mysterious, and because mysterious, it is terrifying and fascinating.

Add to that the impression one experiences when confronted by genuine greatness: in the presence of a tremendous physical upheaval, such as an earthquake or a hurricane; at the sight of something great and beautiful, such as an entire forest ablaze in the glory of autumn colors; at the foot of a great waterfall; or a breathtaking panorama of earth and sea and sky. One feels overwhelmed with a sense of awe. Reporting his impression of the first A-bomb detonation, Brigadier General Farrell wrote:

> We were reaching into the unknown and we did not know what might come of it . . . The whole country was lighted by a searing light with an intensity many times that of the midday sun . . . Thirty seconds after the explosion came, first, the air blast pressing hard against the people and things, to be followed almost immediately by the strong, sustained, awesome roar which warned of doomsday and

made us feel that we puny things were blasphemous to dare tamper with the forces heretofore reserved to the Almighty. Words are inadequate tools for the job of acquainting those not present with the physical, mental and psychological effects. It had to be witnessed to be realized ... The feeling of the entire assembly, even the uninitiated, was one of profound awe.

This, too, is an effect of holiness, the awe which one feels when faced with the overwhelming.

That God, our God, should be so described is not easily accepted by many of us. The holiness of God, this holiness, is not familiar or popular. To many of us God is a kindly, benevolent gentleman who patiently puts up with us and who is always anxious to forgive. He is kind and gentle and there is nothing fearful about Him — let alone something terrible and terrifying. And yet, I speak the truth to you, nothing could be further from the reality. To use Bouyer's phrase, our God is not a "doting grandfather"; He is the Entirely Other, the Holy, the awe-inspiring God of unbearable majesty.

This is the idea of Himself that He has revealed to us in the Bible, if we will only open our eyes to see it. At the risk of overstressing, because it is so important and because without it there is neither understanding nor mystery, I want to offer at least a token sampling of texts in support of this point.

THE TESTIMONY OF SCRIPTURE

Everywhere that God's great power is mentioned, His holiness is implicitly affirmed. He is the Creator, who simply by willing it can call into existence whatever He wishes. He arranges the affairs of men and of nations. He controls the elements and the forces of the world. Throughout and before the exodus He displayed His fearful might, as we have already seen. From the founding of the Hebrew kingdom to its spread and affluence, to its destruction and restoration and, finally, to the sending of the Christ, God made it clear to the Hebrew people that He was their God. From time to time He raised up prophets, often against their will, men who would speak out to remind the people, His chosen people, that He indeed was their God.

There was Isaiah:
    Get behind the rocks,
        hide in the dust,
    From terror of the Lord
        and the splendor of his majesty!
    The haughty eyes of man will be lowered,
        the arrogance of men will be abased,
        and the Lord alone will be exalted, on that day.

(2:10, 11)

And there was Jeremiah:
    The Lord is true God,
        he is the living God, the eternal King,
    Before whose anger the earth quakes,
        whose wrath the nations cannot endure:
    He who made the earth by his power,
        established the world by his wisdom,
        and stretched out the heavens by his skill.

(10:10-12)

Ezechiel wrote of visions of wheels and strange figures beyond human imagination, his way of attesting to the mystery and transcendence of God. Investigating the question of the origin of evil, the book of Job ends, too, with descriptions of weird and unusual things; that is, with the conclusion that God's reasons are beyond our comprehension, simply because God is beyond and above all of creation.

The psalms, too, are a constant witness to awesomeness, the terrifying mystery and majesty of the holy God who is our Creator:

    Serve the Lord with fear, and rejoice before him;
        with trembling pay homage to him,
    Lest he be angry and you perish from the way,
        when his anger blazes suddenly.

(Ps. 2:11, 12)

    For great is the Lord and highly to be praised;
        awesome is he, beyond all gods.
    For all the gods of the nations are things of nought,
        but the Lord made the heavens.

Splendor and majesty go before him;
  praise and grandeur are in his sanctuary.

Give to the Lord, you families of nations,
  give to the Lord glory and praise;
  give to the Lord the glory due his name!
Bring gifts, and enter his courts;
  worship the Lord in holy attire.
Tremble before him, all the earth. . . .

(Ps. 95 (96):4-9)

The Lord is king; the peoples tremble;
  he is throned upon the cherubim; the earth quakes.
The Lord in Zion is great,
  he is high above all the peoples.
Let them praise your great and awesome name;
  holy is he!

(Ps. 98 (99):1-3)

Great is the Lord and highly to be praised;
  his greatness is unsearchable.
Generation after generation praises your works
  and proclaims your might.
They speak of the splendor of your glorious majesty
  and tell of your wondrous works.
They discourse of the power of your terrible deeds
  and declare your greatness.

(Ps. 144 (145):3-6)

I think by now the point is made: God is God. To the believer, the Creator is the Holy One, mysterious, fascinating and terrifying. He is the Entirely Other. Such an understanding of God can produce a profound effect on the way we understand ourselves; but before we attempt to work that out, it must be emphasized that this idea of God was not something that was destined to be altered or discarded with the coming of Christ. God is every bit as much God now as He was before; and the New Testament, too, is eloquent witness of God's holiness.

23

MAN BEFORE GOD

The human response to God's holiness is a mixture of those elements we have already discussed: fear, awe, and fascination. To these must be added reverence, and others which we will come to later. Throughout ancient times and in the Christian era, too, places have been set aside for special worship. They are called shrines or sanctuaries, holy places, for *sanctuary* comes from the Latin word meaning *holy*. The shrines are places which are holy, that is, set aside, set apart for the worship of God who somehow manifested some special sign in that place. Notice that reverence for God extended itself to include things in some way connected with Him. Any display of divine power or visitation from a divine messenger carried with it to the Hebrew believer the implication of God's presence. So it is no wonder that we find Mary, in the New Testament, afraid in the presence of the angel who announced to her that she was to be the mother of the Messiah.

When the birth of Christ was trumpeted by the angels to the shepherds, they threw themselves to the ground and covered their eyes, because they were afraid. Many of the accounts of miracles recorded in the New Testament end with a phrase like: "... and the people were afraid." Perhaps most striking is the account of the Transfiguration in Matthew (17:1-8). Christ took Peter, James, and John up Mount Tabor and was transfigured before them. His countenance was radiant, His garments glowing. Moses and Elias appeared and carried on a conversation with Him. Evidently by this time the Apostles had grown accustomed to seeing Jesus work wonders. They may have been amazed once again, but they were no longer afraid. Peter even made the suggestion that it was good to be there and why not pitch three tents, one for Jesus, one for Moses, and one for Elias. Then, a cloud appeared, the symbol of God's presence ever since the exodus; and a voice thundered from the cloud: "This is my beloved son in whom I am well pleased." At that moment, and not before, Peter, James and John threw themselves to the ground and covered their eyes, because they were afraid.

"Fear of the Lord is the beginning of wisdom," says the Old Testament. The author of the Epistle to the Hebrews wrote:

"... we ... should hold fast to God's grace, through which we may offer worship acceptable to him in reverence and awe. For our God is a consuming fire" (Heb. 12:28, 29). Jesus Himself in many ways and in many parables insisted on the primacy of God, of the need to be concerned about Him above all else. "Seek first his Kingship over you, his way of holiness, and all these things will be given you besides" (Matt. 6:33). The first commandment is to love the Lord your God with your whole heart and your whole soul and your whole mind. And when He taught us to pray, He gave us the words: "Our Father, who are in heaven, hallowed (that is, holy) be thy name... " (Matt. 6:9).

The Christian saints, too, have always recognized God's holiness. St. John Chrysostom, one of the four great Doctors of the Eastern Church, wrote: "We call him the inexpressible, the unthinkable God, the invisible, the inapprehensible; who quells the power of human speech and transcends the grasp of mortal thought; inaccessible to the angels, unbeheld of the seraphim, unimagined of the cherubim, invisible to the principalities and authorities and powers, and in word, to all creation. . . ."

St. Teresa of Avila advised the sisters of her reformed Carmelites that it takes courage to draw near to God. She wrote:

The brilliance of the vision is like that of infused light or of a sun covered with material of the transparency of a diamond, if such a thing could be woven. Almost invariably the soul on which God bestows this favor remains in rapture, because its unworthiness cannot endure so terrible a sight. I say terrible, because though the sight is the loveliest and most delightful imaginable, even by a person who lived and strove to imagine it for a thousand years, because it so far exceeds all that our imagination and understanding can compass, its presence is of such exceeding majesty that it fills the soul with a great terror. It is unnecessary to ask here how, without being told, the soul knows who it is, for He reveals Himself quite clearly as the Lord of Heaven and earth.

The Church, too, perpetuates her awareness of God's holiness in her central act of worship, the renewal of the Sacrifice of Christ, the Sacrifice of the Mass. The solemn moment of consecration is approached slowly and reverently by way of many prayers of preparation and ritual purification; and afterwards there is a gradual, reverent withdrawal. Just before the Canon of the Mass, there is a hymn of thanksgiving and praise, the Preface, which often ends with the formula: "Through whom the angels praise thy majesty, the dominions worship it, the powers tremble...." This is followed by the prayer of the Seraphim in the vision of Isaiah: "Holy, holy, holy, Lord God of hosts. Heaven and earth are full of your glory."

MYSTERY

There it is. The Holy God of Israel is the Holy God of Christianity, and it is only this understanding of God that reveals the mystery of the Hebrew-Christian religion. Why has the Holy God created us? Why does He suffer us? Why has He redeemed us? How could He become a man? Why is He concerned about us? These questions will always remain unanswered, for therein lies the mystery, the mystery of Creation, Incarnation, Redemption and divine love.

The Old and New Testament Scriptures also describe God as Father, Love, Bridegroom, Shepherd, etc., and that is what is so overwhelming. *God, our God,* is our Father! *He* really loves us as a bridegroom! *God, our God,* really *wants* to be known and treated as one who loves us, loves me. He wants to be taken seriously as our God, yet in such a way that we respond to His love for us. How great is His glory! How great His glorious love!

With such an understanding of God, we begin to assume the attitudes of a man of faith. When we finally become aware of the supreme majesty and overwhelming splendor of the God who dwells in unapproachable light, we cannot help but feel unworthy and sinful and insignificant. We begin to understand how the saints could say of themselves: "I am unworthy. I am nothing. I am a sinner." We begin to realize that this evaluation of themselves sprang, not from a morbid self-depreciation, but from a vivid awareness of the reality of God.

When a man stands at the shore of a great sea, contemplating its vastness, he cannot help but feel small and

26

insignificant. And when he extends his vision to the wide reaches of space and the huge galaxies which expand throughout it, he may very well come to the conclusion, as others have, that he is but a speck of cosmic dust. Now let his vision go beyond even that to the Holy God who is its Creator, whose splendor and majesty are but dimly reflected in all of this, His creation — what are his feelings then? In a word, he feels humble, for humility is the awareness and acceptance of one's own nothingness, sinfulness and unworthiness before God.

PERSPECTIVE

When illumined by the Light of the world and confronted by Him who created heaven and earth, we begin to understand ourselves for what we really are. We can no longer accept the illusion that we have made ourselves into something quite worthwhile. There comes a moment, a brief instant at least, when, exposed to the sudden realization of what God is and finally secured in the grip of that experience, we become transparent to ourselves. We understand our utter insignificance and our defilement.

And, as we become more and more penetrated by the idea of His divinity, as we begin to understand more clearly and appreciate more fully the content of the words, "My God," at the same time we gain an insight and a perspective which lights up our whole existence. All of reality becomes transformed before our eyes. We see with the clear vision of a man who has been elevated to the vantage point of God. All ordinary standards of judgment fall like scales from our eyes and we see. We see ourselves and our world and everything in it for what they undoubtedly are. We know with unshakeable certitude that this is God's world and that it is nothing.

UNITY

The realization of the holiness of God is elevating and liberating. Our day-to-day, humdrum dullness and bluntness are shattered by the intrusion of a reality that cannot be ignored or silenced. For once, for the moment, we understand — and it seems as though we understand everything. All of a sudden everything in existence falls into place. We know what we are, what the world is, what everything in the world is for. The multiplicity of our experience, which has always served to confuse and distract us, has been reduced to unity. At once we see all things in God.

This, too, is another human reaction to the Holy: the sense of *unity* with God, the sense of identification. In *The Varieties of Religious Experience,* William James writes: "The perfect stillness of the night was thrilled by a more solemn silence. The darkness held a presence that was all the more felt because it was not seen. I could not anymore have doubted that *He* was there than that I was. Indeed, I felt myself to be, if possible, the less real of the two." And a little later: "What I felt on these occasions was a temporary loss of my own identity."

We are body, soul, and spirit, made in the image of God. God is rational and free — and mystery — and so are we. The Father loves the Son and this life and love and power which goes back and forth between Them is the Spirit *(ruah* or *pneuma).* But that Spirit flows from the Father through the Son and His Body, through *us* and back to Him. To the degree to which we have been broken, really turned over to Him — to that degree His life, His Spirit lives in us and flows back to the Father in worship. In this way we share in His nature, His life! To be holy, then, does not consist in doing a lot of religious things, but in a sharing in God's own holiness, God's own Holy Spirit. To be a Christian, filled with the Spirit, is this unbelievable Good News: that we share in the life and power and immortality of God Himself!

PRAYER

Finally, a word about prayer. Prayer is a form of communication, a being-present-with-God. In some ways it is hard for people to understand this because so few people really know how to be present to another. We speak without responding, we hear without listening, we look without seeing. Our minds, our attention is so often other than where we are. To be present to another means more than exchanging sentences or customary gestures. It is to sense the *who* beyond the *what*, the *someone* without boxes.

Praying begins when we become present to God, when we enter into the Sacred, when we become present to the loving majesty and tender person of the God who is God. Entering into prayer does not begin until we realize into whose presence we have come. More about this in a later chapter.

BIBLIOGRAPHY

RECOMMENDED READING:

Evely, Louis, *Teach Us How to Pray,* Paulist-Newman, Paramus, New Jersey, 1973, 106pp.
Especially helpful in showing you how to let God reveal Himself to you in prayer instead of your making speeches to God.

SUPPLEMENTARY READING:

Evely, Louis, *Credo,* Sheed and Ward, London, 1967, 179pp.
A personally challenging meditation on the Creed. The first three chapters are especially helpful for the topic we have considered in this chapter.

Otto, Rudolf, *The Idea of the Holy,* Oxford Press, New York, New York, 1923, 232pp.
The primary reference for this chapter. It is a scholarly and thorough treatment of the experience of the mystery or "otherness" of God.

by Tony Cushing

Jesus: The Man and the Mission

To experience what salvation means is to experience the intimate love of Jesus. There is no way around it. To enter the Kingdom of Heaven is fundamentally to have something happen to you. And what happens is simply that you accept that Jesus personally loves you. You begin a loving relationship with Jesus which gradually changes you into a lover like Him.

Now, to have a living relationship with someone presupposes that you have met him and experienced his love. This is very different from *knowing about* a person. For instance, I might have a friend whom I love deeply. Maybe I talk about him a lot. You might learn a great deal about my friend from me — how he talks, what's important to him, what he looks like. But no matter how much information you have, you wouldn't say that you love my friend. You might admire him the way you'd admire a president or a war hero. But love could come only through a personal encounter and a continued shared experience with that person. Just think of what happens when two people start dating so that a loving relationship can grow. Love is different from having information about someone. Love is an experienced relationship shared with a person present to me.

Obviously the question here is: "How is God present to us?" or "How do we encounter Him?" Before I attempt to answer that, we have to acknowledge that our religious education has given most of us a measure of *information about God.* Generally, few of us have been taught to *expect* a personal encounter and relationship with Jesus. So, before we talk about how to come to know Jesus, we have to clear up a few misconceptions about who Jesus is and how to relate to Him.

In our first chapter we described salvation in terms of the Father sending the Son to let us know that we are perfectly loved and known. To experience this love is to enter the process of being saved. To talk about how this happens, I have to describe how it happened to me. There are a number of reasons for doing this. First of all, I am not just talking about a theory to be analyzed. I am sharing the most important thing in my life — the person whose love has changed me to the very depths of my person. Secondly, it means that something beautiful has happened to me and many others, and that we can all expect a similar change in our own lives. And as you look for and expect Jesus to relate to you in this way, then you can be receptive or open to His love. It's a lot like taking the cover off the dinner tray. The food was always there, it's just that now you can eat it. We all need to take the covers away from the love of Jesus. To see the way in which someone else accepted His love can help us to have faith to experience this also.

A third reason is that personal experience has always been the context of talking about a relationship with Jesus. He is

> what we have seen with our eyes,
> what we have looked upon
> and our hands have touched—
> What we have seen and heard
> we proclaim in turn to you
> so that you may share life with us.

(1 John 1:2, 3)

Jesus promised the disciples that they would be "filled with power from on high" so that they could be "my witnesses in Jerusalem, throughout Judea and Samaria, yes, even to the ends of the earth" (Acts 1:8). For all of these reasons it is necessary to talk about what happened between me and Jesus. Also it just so happens that I like to do this simply because He loves me and has made me happy.

PERSONAL TESTIMONY

I was raised in a lower middle-class parish where I went to the Catholic elementary school. As the youngest child and only boy, I was quite the spoiled brat. Consequently at a very early age I developed a talent for being self-righteous, which simultaneously astounded and enraged my teachers. I was also precocious in the manly art of skepticism. At the age of seven or eight I was a convinced empiricist. I literally had see to believe. This conflicted with my religious education in the 3rd grade when our nun was describing the properties of guardian angels. She even said that my guardian angel could be sitting in my chair! Being at that time a very chubby little boy who even overlapped the chair, I knew there was no room for any angel in my seat. You see, at the time I had not read Aquinas' discourse on the number of angels on the head of a pin. As a result, I relegated the sister's religion to the realm of amusing fairytales.

This early attitude lasted into high school; there I challenged the priests to prove the existence of God. In this manner I was an agent for the increase of the virtue of patience in many holy men. And I was consistently amazed at how these apparently intelligent men could be so foolish as to believe in God. At this point I was convinced that if God existed, He certainly didn't do anything for me except cause a lot of problems and nasty rules. Yet, in spite of this practical atheism, I would still go to confession, which had made me "feel good" since age seven.

College was much the same progression — I learned lots about God. He was an interesting intellectual problem which was easy to discuss since it had nothing to do with real life. Real life was absurd and depressing, facts which led to a few hilarious failures at suicide and eventually prompted one of my theology professors to recommend a retreat. I went, hoping to have a "four-day high" from the sensitivity techniques, but instead was challenged to give my life to Jesus. I thought this was a lot of naive garbage. But as I started to really look at my life, I saw that while I was intelligent, successful in drama, with lots of good friends, I still didn't believe that anyone really loved me for myself. At the time, we were in the chapel and people were getting too emotional for me; I mean this was too serious for tears. If all my talents didn't make people love me, then what would? Eventually I was left alone in despair in this chapel of a God who didn't exist. And for some reason I knelt down and felt foolish; then I even more foolishly prostrated myself, and

33

gradually I knew He was there. This Jesus was saying, "But I know you, I know everything about you and I love you." That was it! I just started smiling and talking to Him and smiling. I was loved even though I had ignored the lover for so long, and, if He loved me now, that meant He would always love me.

This basic relationship has stayed with me. Jesus is my friend who knows me completely. So I talk to Him a lot. He's with me in the car and I can just share with Him what I feel like. He speaks to me in many ways (Bible, prayer, people, nature) and challenges me to be free, to be myself. He comforts me when I'm down on myself. Most of all, He loves me when I feel no one else could love me. He's not only my brother but He's my Lord, the King of Creation, and so I can trust that giving my life to Him works. He knows what is best for me much more than I do. He's my God, who made me and will hopefully one day share all He has with me — even though I ignored Him.

So that is why all of this talk about getting to know who Jesus is makes sense to me. I've met Jesus and He is simply the most important person in my life. Also, I've developed a modest belief in angels; even though I'm still as chubby, and they still don't fit on the chair. Reading Aquinas really did help. But enough about me — I'd rather talk about Jesus.

THE MAN JESUS

Some people read the Gospels hoping to find out a lot about the biography of Jesus. They are usually disappointed. There is no physical description of Jesus; His early life is generally unreported, His personal tastes and cultural preferences are unknown. All of the things that would interest us in the "story of a great man" are missing — Why? First of all we have to look into the purpose of the Gospel writers.

What we have seen and heard we tell to you also, so that you will join with us in the fellowship that we have with the Father and with his Son Jesus Christ. (1 John 1:3 — TEV)

Scripture is the witness of the Church, of its encounter with Jesus. The evangelists weren't trying to prove that a man Jesus existed — they already knew that and so did the Christian communities. Their purpose was to increase the faith of the people ("join with us in fellowship"), not to satisfy the investigations of a historian. This is not to downgrade biographical investigations. It merely means that history and biography were not what the Gospel writers were primarily concerned with. As John McKenzie explains:

... the purpose of the authors was not to write a life but to *present the object of the Christian faith and preaching.* The object which they presented *was* the real historical person Jesus Christ, but they did not and were unable to present His historical biography. Even the personality of Jesus, it seems, was not the primary object of interest.... We can believe that the atmosphere of mystery in which He appears reflects the atmosphere of His historic presence; those who knew Him and related the ancedotes from which the Gospels were written knew that there were depths in Him which they never comprehended. The modern historian will do well to respect their reserve. *(Dictionary of the Bible* p. 432, Italics mine)

It's almost as if the humanity of Jesus is taken for granted. This makes sense, since the witnesses were those who had lived with Him, eaten with Him and shared His everyday life. It's much the same kind of attitude you would take in describing a beautiful room. You would relate what makes the room beautiful — the fact that there was a floor would be assumed and unreported. The Gospel writers were trying to witness to what makes Jesus the Lord, not so much what made Him man.

All of this is fine, but it doesn't fulfill our 20th century need to know Jesus as man. The man who walked in Galilee. We need to be able to relate to this man Jesus. If not, what was the purpose of the Incarnation? Jesus was "a man like us in all things but sin" (Eucharistic Prayer IV). What did people see when they encountered Jesus?

To answer this we have to realize that many of the popular ideas we have about Jesus are products of a couple of thousand years of holy imagination. For example, most of the pictures of Jesus from my childhood portrayed Jesus with blonde hair, blue eyes, pink cheeks and a sort of glow all around Him. That was the Polish version. Almost every culture depicts Jesus with the particular racial characteristics and physical attitudes fashionable at the time. I've even seen a picture of Jesus in knight's armor. Most of this is an attempt to make Jesus "a man like us in all things," except that often we wander pretty far from the real man of the first century. In my background Jesus came off as the most effeminate-looking man I ever saw. I really didn't want to know someone who looked like that. So what we need to do is to somehow pierce through the rosy haze with which well-meaning Christian piety has clouded the picture of Jesus. To do this the only tools we have are bits of Scripture, our imagination and the everyday realities of first-century Palestine. Creating a mental picture of the man Jesus is one of the oldest and most successful techniques in meditative prayer (i.e., rosary, stations of the cross).

THE CARPENTER FROM NAZARETH

A good place to begin is John the Baptist's statement, "There is one among you whom you do not recognize" (John 1:26). Just this one line should be enough to convince us that there was nothing physically or intellectually remarkable about Jesus. First of all, He is "among us," participating in everything human beings normally do. Secondly, He does this in such a way that people can't see anything unusual; they "do not recognize" anything special in Him. For thirty years He was among us unnoticed.

Think of God the Almighty as a baby. First of all He was brought up like other children. By this I mean that He had to learn how to walk, talk and play just like all children have to do. He grew up in a small Jewish village, went to the synagogue, learned the Scriptures. Hopefully He learned how to make friends with the other kids in town. All in all, quite ordinary. "He grew up in age and wisdom." Try to think of Jesus around ten years old playing with the other children, doing everyday errands. He probably fumbled around with Joseph's tools, trying to act like a grown-up. As an adolescent, perhaps He was more than a little clumsy (as most of us were). And as Jesus grew older, there must have been some speculation among the relatives about when He would get married.

Imagine what Jesus looked like. First of all, how tall is He? Our first reaction is to think of looking up into Jesus' eyes. But actually, with nutrition and everything being what it was, men weren't that tall back then. I think they averaged around 5'5". So suppose Jesus was tall, around 5'10". Well I'm 6'3". That means that Jesus would come up to about my nose. How about His face, His complexion? Being a Jew He would be rather dark, and years in the sun would have made His skin leathery. This was no pale-faced, rosy-cheeked Jesus, but a rough country Jew. Perhaps He even had pock-marks from disease (no vaccinations then). And how about His hair? Black and curly, cut with shears and not often. Jesus was perhaps not very clean according to our antiseptic standards. And at that time racial characteristics must have been very pronounced, so include a rather large hooked nose and probably thick dark lips. More Asian than European, more brown than white, Jesus probably looked like the average poor Israelite.

What about Jesus' voice? Our first reaction might be to think of Jesus having a very gentle, yet resonant voice that just had to touch your heart, like the cultured actor who plays Him in the movies. We have to remember that Jesus came from the hill country and had a distinctive accent. It was distinctive because Galileans spoke with a kind of slurring lisp which was immediately evident to the urbane Jerusalemites. The way most New Yorkers would react to a pronounced southern drawl is probably the way city people reacted to Jesus. He was a hillbilly to them.

As a carpenter, Jesus' hands were probably scarred and rough. Our God had callouses, and His feet were probably beaten and dirty from much walking. So what did people see when they saw Jesus? They saw Him for what He was — an average-looking Jew, rather rough and homespun — a poor, backwoods preacher from an unpopular part of the country. "One among you whom you do not recognize."

Some people are sure to think that imagining Jesus in this way would be almost sacriligious. Yet, the only part of Scripture which could possibly describe the physical appearance of Jesus (personally I don't think it does) is a much bleaker picture in the servant-songs of Isaiah:

Who would believe what we have heard?
... There was in him no stately bearing
  to make us look at him,
nor appearance that would attract us to him.
... One of those from whom men hide their faces. ...

(Isaiah 53:1-3)

We have a tendency to think of Jesus as inhumanly beautiful, and some people would cut Him off from everyday human life. But, realistically, why wouldn't Jesus have had pimples as an adolescent or work up a sweat or, for that matter, not smell so sweet? Saying this does not mean that we lose our reverence or awe for Jesus. After all, that's the way God chose to reveal Himself — poor and weak, hidden in our flesh. The more of a man Jesus is, the more profound is His divinity. Think of how we relate to a king or a millionaire who keeps a safe distance from ordinary men — hidden behind his status. We respect him in his proper role. But if a king goes about once in a while in everyday clothes like us — not only do we still respect him, but because he accepts the everyday life, we refer to him as a "regular guy." "Came right up and talked to me, he did." Well it's the same with Jesus. He's the prince who became a pauper. God is also a regular guy who will talk with us and share our everyday life with us.

THE SON OF MAN

Have you ever thought that believing in Jesus is really difficult now, but that if only you could have seen Him in His time, performing a miracle or healing someone — why, then you would have believed? Have you ever wondered why the whole of first-century Judaism didn't convert en masse when Jesus appeared. Well, let's look at how easy it would have been to recognize the man Jesus as anything but the Son of God.

One time He went back home and proclaimed that He was the Messiah whom Isaiah had foretold as "anointed to proclaim the good news to the poor." He got at best, mixed reviews.

They were filled with amazement, and said to one another,

"Where did this man get such wisdom and miraculous powers? Isn't this the carpenter's son? Isn't Mary known to be his mother and James, Joseph, Simon and Judas his brothers? Aren't his sisters our neighbors? Where did he get all this?" They found him altogether too much for them.

(Matt. 13:54-57)

Would you have recognized Jesus? Here is this man Josue bar Joseph from Nazareth, carpenter by trade, little or no formal education, a poor laborer who speaks with a lisp, announcing: "Repent, the Kingdom of God is at hand . . . I am the Way, the Truth and the Life." As Isaiah said, "Who would believe what we have heard?"

Not only that, but look at the people He associated with — sinners, tax collectors, prostitues, fishermen. Hardly the in-crowd for the status seekers. It's hard to figure out who He was trying to impress with all these outcasts hanging around. "The Son of Man came and he both ate and drank, and you say, 'Here is a glutton and a drunkard, a friend of tax collectors and sinners' " (Luke 7:34). An average man followed by the average, unruly, fickle mob. He even sat down to dinner with public sinners and self-admitted thieves.

Imagine you were a stranger trying to find Jesus in Jerusalem. If you asked the first-century equivalent to a big city cabbie, you might get something like this for an answer: "Well, in the daytime check the temple. If he's not there, look for a crowd, and watch yourself, bud, them's not respectable people. If not there, try the slums — but you'll have to get somebody else to take you there. And every once in a while the whole troop goes off to parks and hillsides for some kind of picnic, though most of the time they forget to bring anything to eat. And if worse come to worse, ask one of the Pharisees; they usually got a fix on him."

And consider the kinds of things this supposed rabble-rouser says: "Before Abraham was, I am." "Unless you eat my flesh and drink my blood, you'll not enter into the kingdom. . . ." Can't you sympathize with the befuddled Pharisees in this passage:

Jesus spoke to them once again:

"I am the light of the world.
No follower of mine shall ever walk in darkness;
no, he shall possess the light of life."

This caused the Pharisees to break in with: "You are your own witness. Such testimony cannot be valid." Jesus answered:
"What if I am my own witness?
My testimony is valid nonetheless,
because I know where I came from
and where I am going;
you know neither the one nor the other.
You pass judgment according to appearances
but I pass judgment on no man.
Even if I do judge,
that judgment of mine is valid
because I am not alone:
I have at my side the One who sent me [the Father].
It is laid down in your law
that evidence given by two persons is valid.
I am one of those testifying in my behalf,
the Father who sent me is the other."

They pressed him: "And where is this 'Father' of yours?" Jesus replied:

"You know neither me nor my Father.
If you knew me, you would know my Father too."

He spoke these words while teaching at the temple treasury. Still, he went unapprehended, because his hour had not yet come.

(John 8:12-20)

St. John's closing comment leads one to surmise that most people would be arrested for speeches like that simply because it was so frustrating. "The man just ain't logical." The Pharisees ask really down-to-earth, practical questions, and they seem to get the runaround. One of my friends commented that in this incident, he probably would have sided with the Pharisees. Jesus seemed too much the egomaniac. He just asked too much to be accepted on faith. Why wouldn't He tell us who or where this

Father was? Jesus seemed to use Him as the solution to all questions; why didn't He supply the concrete answers?

A STUMBLING BLOCK

This is "the foolish message we preach" (I Cor. 1:21 — TEV), Jesus Christ, "the stumbling block" whom Kierkegaard says was a "sign of contradiction" to the people of his time. What this means is that you either had to accept Jesus totally for what He said He was, or you rejected Him and were offended by what He said. There was no middle ground. If you really understood that He claimed to be the "Son of Man" and said, "I am who I am" (which means *Yahweh)*, then you couldn't think He was just a good man, or a fine example. Either He was God or He was crazy and needed to be put away. "He blasphemes," the priests said, and in any other case they would have been right. How would you respond if a man said he was God? One time in Galilee, His family came to fetch Him home because the people were saying, "He's gone mad." His opponents tried to arrest Him, to make a fool of Him. At least three times they tried to stone Him, but He got away because His hour had not yet come.

What made it even more offensive was that He wasn't even the first to claim to be the Messiah. The Jews were in a fever pitch of expectancy, so there were frequent appearances of new messiahs from the countryside. As Gamaliel told the Jewish Council:

Not long ago a certain Theudas came on the scene and tried to pass himself off as someone of importance . . . . However he was killed, and all those who had been so easily convinced by him were disbanded. In the end it came to nothing. Next came Judas the Galilean at the time of the census. He too built up quite a following, but likewise died, and all of his followers were dispersed. The present case is similar.

(Acts 5:36-38)

It was standard procedure for the Pharisees to sally forth to trip up these supposed messiahs with trick questions. When they proved the aspirant a sham, the crowd would stone him. It was all very routine. And they apparently expected the same with

41

Jesus. Except for the surprises of the resurrection and Pentecost, they were right.

Yet in all of this, there was obviously something which attracted people to Jesus. Huge crowds did follow Him and even try to make Him king. Respectable people and Pharisees invited Him into their homes so that they could listen to this new rabbi. "Jesus . . . left the crowds spellbound at his teaching. The reason was that he taught with authority and not like their scribes" (Mt. 7:28-29). This authority was His union with the author of the Law, the Father. People experienced this in His obvious holiness. He lived what He spoke about. Jesus said, "Forgive seventy times seventy." Can't you imagine Peter constantly boasting and Jesus constantly forgiving him, accepting him in love. And the way He treated sinners, loving them in a manner that changed their lives. Think of how the people who really encountered Him must have talked about Him to their friends. "Why, not only was I healed of the palsy, but he said that my sins were forgiven. You know, I really felt forgiven, I felt like a new person — clean and new." Add to this all of the miracles, healings, people being raised from the dead. Not everyone believed in these even when they were done in front of their eyes. Some even said He did these things through the power of the devil. But, really, what kind of a person would stand up in the synagogue and ask the Pharisees if it were allowable to heal on the Sabbath and then cure a man's withered arm right in front of them?

Jesus was a man. A bold, courageous, forceful man who awed people with the power of love. I can't imagine some effeminate milksop driving the money changers out of the temple with a whip. Here was a new rabbi with a message old and new. The poor people loved him. After all, He was poor, and He gave them the hope of a new kind of life. Here He was, this new rabbi, who loved, wept, laughed, sang and was at home with practically everyone. (He appears to be also the most peaceful celebrity who ever lived.) He manifested a real power to love and heal. People brought the sick to Him from miles around — "All of Syria heard about him" — a miracle-worker who didn't terrify or try to impress, but seemed to take this power for granted and was more interested in persons. He was a person who was good news.

JESUS' EFFECT ON PEOPLE

How would we have reacted to Jesus had we lived in His time? To help us do that, I want to present a few stories about how everyday people might have reacted to Jesus. Imagine a typical family in Galilee. The father is a hard-working fisherman, and after years of sacrifice and with the help of his two sons, he has succeeded in building up a respectable fleet. It's a good, stable life. They even have a few luxuries which the father loves to share with his once beautiful wife. Except for taxes, the Romans don't bother them. Surrounded by good old neighbors and friends, they also have a reputation for generosity to the poor and hospitality. The father is rough and boisterous, but everyone knows he's really soft-hearted. The mother is the real strength of the family. Passionately religious in a quiet way, she has instilled the family with a sense of the rightness of the Jewish faith. Holy days are real celebrations and the Sabbath is observed to the letter. And the sons, after a brief period of rebelliousness, have, through her influence, seen the goodness of this quiet, ordered life. They expect to marry, to carry on this tradition of hard work, friendliness and age-old faith. It's an honest, manly life with a place for everyone and everyone in his place.

But something happens while visiting a relative. The oldest son's betrothed goes to listen to this new preacher, Jesus of Nazareth, and she is excited and challenged by his unusual message of love. She had even seen him heal a crippled man and he had said, "Your sins are forgiven," and it seemed that this had really happened to the man. Suddenly there are a lot more possibilities to life. She shares this with her fiance, and out of respect for her, he is curious, wanting to know more. He had always suspected there was more to life, but everything he had tried turned out to be a disappointment.

He starts to talk with his brother about it. Eventually it becomes part of the dinner conversation. "Do you think that the Messiah will come in our time?" "Is it sacriligious to heal on the Sabbath?" "Did you hear that he said we were to love our enemies?" The father is confused and feels somewhat threatened. "Life is good enough without these holy men rocking the boat. Why didn't he stay in the desert? And what about that line, 'Look at the birds in the sky. They do not sow or reap?' Well, if he had a family to feed, he'd be whistling a different tune. And a man is to leave his father and mother to follow him, huh! Well, who does he think he is? He's undermining the family structure, teaching people to loaf. I don't care how many miracles he did; you just can't throw tradition and responsibility out the window. Well, the Pharisees will show him what's what." He eventually forbids discussing Jesus at the table.

But the mother sees the father's objection for what it is — a fear of change. She too feels this, yet her lifetime of devotion has made her realize that faith is a matter of the heart, of loving God. The words, "unless you become like little children," have meaning for her, since she performed the rituals and externals of the faith with a child's simplicity. It was the only way she knew how to love God. And now Jesus claims we can say, "Our Father." She sees that this trust and love is the only thing that makes a family possible. She finds in Jesus the fulfillment of the law she's tried so hard to keep. She is burdened and heavily ladened with the family and with everyday life. She alone of the whole family recognizes her need for Jesus and need for love. But she has obligations to her husband. She can't just run away like a young girl or like those prostitutes. She has always been faithful, and it was a great effort to do so since she could have had other men. "Why did Jesus seem to accept that adulterous woman?" It was like a slap in the face to respectable women like her. Was all of her effort for nothing? If she merely desired someone in her heart, this Jesus said that that was just as bad as adultery. "Well, that was too much — isn't keeping the law enough?" And so she battles with accepting Jesus — stops talking about him to keep peace with the father. Once in a while during the day she stops and daydreams about what it would be like if everything this man said were really true. Love and friendship. Our Father! Our Father. No, it just wouldn't work; people were against him. Maybe her husband was right; maybe he does upset things too much. In almost accepting Jesus, she becomes the most bitter of the whole family toward him and occasionally talks against him with the other women.

How would the priests have reacted to Jesus? They had the law, they were trying to do God's will insofar as they knew it. And here comes another preacher. He challenges them to change, to repent like anyone else, like a sinner. He calls them "a brood of vipers," "hyprocrites and whitewashed tombs." Well, if that's the way he's going to treat the respectable religious people. . . . Yet the priests and Pharisees were always hanging around Jesus, probably to trip him up. Maybe a few were cut to the heart and actually did repent. Some of these couldn't publicly follow Jesus like Nicodemus; it was too socially unacceptable. "I mean, if only the man would make a few compromises, accommodate himself to those in power — I'm sure they would recognize him." But the risk was probably too great. Jesus undermined the established order of religion. He upset too many of the righteous and respectable.

"The Romans would think they had another revolution on their hands. Can't he keep his followers quiet about this 'king' business?" Then, in the end, it was "better that one man should die for the sake of the nation."

There were the political activists, the zealots who wanted to overthrow the Romans rule. Here is a man who had the crowds in the palm of his hand. Sure he was ordinary, but there would be no problem making him king. Once again, religion and the army would be united in a new David. Why did he refuse them, "give to Caesar the things that are Caesar's"? He's really becoming a milksop now. Come on, Jesus, you said, "Not peace but a sword." Vindicate God's people, strike down our enemies. More and more as the message becomes trust in the Father and "the Son of Man must suffer and die," the political activists turn away from this holy dreamer.

So it went, people came to Jesus expecting Him to act as their Messiah would act. But Jesus was always a surprise. He had no programs of political action or social renewal. "Come, follow me" was what He said. Some people in this encounter with love were really changed. Others became disappointed and left: "This saying is too hard." Jesus just defies people's categories. He wasn't a rebel, nor was He an establishment man. He was a religious revolutionary who displayed an amazing lack of the wisdom of the world and sometimes lacked what would seem to be ordinary common sense. He offended the powerful and rejoiced in the weak. The man just didn't have any tact, and He almost always did what shrewdness would call the wrong thing to win friends and influence people. Jesus continually resists all efforts of men to pin Him down to a safe and predictable person. He is perpetually the square peg in the round hole. This is the mystery of His personality that McKenzie talked about. Jesus is infinitely discoverable, always a surprise. He is the quintessential person who is the encounter of mystery, of the living God.

It's the same today. Jesus is still a "sign of contradiction," "the stumbling block." He is still mysteriously Himself. And He still says, "Come to me, all you who are heavy-burdened and I will give you rest." It's still an act of personal faith to accept Jesus as He is. He came not for "peace but the sword," the sword of truth in accepting Him. Some will and some won't, and even families will be split in accepting or rejecting Him. What we are left with is a choice — "either we're for Him or we're against Him." Either we accept all of His claims as to who He was or we owe Him the decency to reject Him completely and not make Him in our own image. And He still says:

> How I wish you were one or the other — hot or cold! But because you are lukewarm, neither hot nor cold, I will spew you out of my mouth!...Here I stand, knocking at the door. If anyone hears me calling and opens the door, I will enter his house and have supper with him, and he with me.
>
> (Rev. 3:15, 16, 20)

THE MISSION OF JESUS

Renewing the sense of the humanity of Jesus helps us to understand the totality of the personal decision to which He challenged people. In so emphasizing the difficulty of recognizing the Son of God, I have perhaps made Jesus more of a scandal than He actually was. Regardless, we do know that the political and religious establishment had to eliminate Him because He was such a threat. What we need to do now is to look at what Jesus' life, death, and resurrection mean for us now. Obviously I can't cover this in anywhere near the depth that it needs (at least several volumes). I do want to relate some of the basic ways Jesus has meaning for me and maybe start you thinking about different aspects of the God-man, Jesus.

"God is one.
One also is the mediator between God and men,
the man Christ Jesus,
who gave himself as a ransom for all."

(I Timothy 2:5, 6)

St. Paul also says that Jesus is "the visible likeness of the invisible God." And Jesus says that when "you see me you see the Father." Jesus is what God is like. What He says is that God is a Father who is love. The Creator wants only good things for you. Rejoice, life is a lot more hopeful than your wildest dreams, because the Father loves you.

Jesus went out to announce the Good News that the Kingdom of God was at hand. There is no more need to be anxious, for the Father knows our needs and loves us. The Christ is the "anointed one" sent by the Father:

"The spirit of the Lord is upon me;
therefore he has anointed me.
He has sent me to bring glad tidings to the poor,
to proclaim liberty to captives,
Recovery of sight to the blind
and release to prisoners,
To announce a year of favor from the Lord."

(Luke 4:18, 19)

Jesus' very name *(Josue or Joshuah)* means *Yahweh's salvation* (revealed), and it's news almost too good to be true. Isn't what Jesus announced what all of us deep down want to hear? Life with all of its suffering is really a comedy; it all works out because God is a Father (Our Father) who loves us.

This Good News was not only what Jesus said but what He did and who He was. The Good News was healing for the sick,

47

deliverance for the oppressed and, most of all, forgiveness and love. We are no longer cut off from the Holy One whom to see is to die, but "God is with us." We're OK. This is what *Savior* and *Christ* mean; we are now put right with God.

THE SUFFERING SERVANT

Not only is God revealed in the man Jesus, the poor man who shares our life with us, but the way Yahweh's salvation is accomplished is through weakness and suffering and death. Jesus "sacrifices himself to win freedom for all mankind." He is the suffering servant (or slave) of Yahweh:

He was spurned and avoided by men,
     a man of suffering, accustomed to infirmity,
One of those from whom men hide their faces,
     spurned, and we held him in no esteem.

Yet it was our infirmities that he bore,
     our sufferings that he endured,
While we thought of him as stricken,
     as one smitten by God and afflicted.
But he was pierced for our offenses,
     crushed for our sins;
Upon him was the chastisement that makes us whole,
     by his stripes we were healed.
We had all gone astray like sheep,
     each following his own way;
But the Lord laid upon him
     the guilt of us all.

Though he was harshly treated, he submitted
     and opened not his mouth;
Like a lamb led to the slaughter
     or a sheep before the shearers,
     he was silent and opened not his mouth.
Oppressed and condemned, he was taken away,
     and who would have thought any more of his destiny?
When he was cut off from the land of the living,
     and smitten for the sin of his people. . . .

And he shall take away the sins of many,
and win pardon for their offenses.

(Isaiah 53:3-8, 12)

It is precisely in this that God proves his love for us:
that while we were still sinners, Christ died for us.

(Romans 5:8)

What does it mean to say that Jesus died for me in love? This is the very heart of the Good News. Christ has died. Alleluia! And He did it to take away my guilt, my isolation — to prove this love which risks everything for me.

To meditate on the passion of Christ is very graphically to realize the suffering and pain that an innocent man chose to endure as a gift for us. Here was the "man without sin" arrested without justice. Completely cut off and misunderstood, He cries out, "Why do you look for a chance to kill me?" (John 7:19). Man's hostility to love comes to a head in the injustice of condemning Jesus who is love. And this is no heroic and grand rebel defending his innocence. He is defenseless like the lamb. Jesus rejects all power and coercion while He is subject to all earthly power. He is the poor man totally oppressed, controlled by the hatred of the world.

And He suffers as every man must suffer. He does not like the pain. He prays that there could be another way, but there isn't. He is taken, bound and mocked as any ignorant peasant would be. People even spit in his face. He becomes the animal that men make of each other, stripped of dignity and respect. So they scourge Him the way they scourged every animal. Roman whips were the epitome of crime deterrent. They had long leather thongs tipped with hooks or bits of metal to tear the flesh. The method was to whip over the back so as to catch the hooks in the flesh and then pull it off. Jesus got the maximum 39 lashes. They had to stop there or else the prisoner would die. And so the mobs who once cheered Him as Messiah accepted into their midst a convicted murderer, Barabbas, so that this half-dead Jesus could be cursed on the cross as the King of the Jews.

There is a routine cruelty to crucifixion which numbs a person like the horrors of Auschwitz. Nails are driven through the flesh in the wrists in such a way that they press against the major nerves to the hand. And nails go through the feet, crushing the bones and blood vessels. A crucified person died of asphyxiation, and often it took days to die. Eventually the man's arms and legs grew weak and he slumped down, pressing the collar bones into his throat, cutting off the air. Then he would have to force himself up to breathe, only to collapse again in exhaustion until he simply had no strength left. He would turn pink and then blue as he died in front of everyone. They called this struggle for breath, "the dance of the crucified." Jesus was, I suppose, fortunate that He had only three hours to struggle this dance. So He hung there writhing and naked as people taunted Him to finally be like their God and save Himself and come down from the cross.

The physical suffering was nothing compared to the psychological and spiritual suffering that Jesus had to undergo. He had seen the crowds leave Him and had even asked if His apostles would leave Him also, which they did. A close friend betrays Him and His protege denies that he ever knew Him. He was deserted and left alone by those He loved. Here is where He loved the most. If you ever had a friend betray your trust, you know how much that hurts. The depth of Jesus' love is seen in the way He treats Peter. Kierkegaard comments on the passage where Jesus looks at Peter in the High Priest's courtyard. Jesus knows what Peter has done. Some people might think that it would have been manly for Jesus to stare Peter down — make him know how disgusting his action had been — scorn him. Others would say that it would have been noble for Jesus to turn the other way, not to let Peter know He saw him. Kierkegaard says that Jesus looked at Peter in the way a mother would look at her child who is playing dangerously close to a cliff. She doesn't scream or even move for fear that she'll startle the child into falling. She looks at the child with love as if to draw him to herself. So Jesus looks at Peter with love, as if to say, "I still forgive you, I still love you, I still accept you." And Peter turned away and wept bitterly.

HE BECAME SIN

Jesus was always alone, the good man among sinners. He was constantly misunderstood, denied and insulted throughout His public life. The passion condensed all of this isolation into a moment to total rejection by mankind. There is more than this. Paul says that Jesus became sin on the cross (2 Cor. 5:21). He not only bore our guilt and substituted Himself for our punishment, He became sin — total isolation, totally alone and abandoned by everyone, even His Father. This is understood by some theologians to be the complete emptying of self (Phil. 2:17). When Jesus prayed the psalm, "My God, my God, why have you forsaken me?" it seems that even the Father withdrew His presence from Him. The Father with whom He was completely one somehow withdrew from Jesus so that He might become totally isolated — the forsaken one become sin. It was then, in the abyss of despair, that Jesus chose to love: "Father forgive them, they know not what they do." And so He died as men die but in order to set us free.

I'm not writing this to be morbid or to stir up feelings of guilt. I'm writing this because it happens to be the way it happened. It is grotesque, but it was common for the times. It's so disgusting that one doctor who wrote of the physical aspects of Calvary wonders why, when people say the stations of the cross, they aren't completely nauseated in horror. The suffering is real, but what is amazing is that Jesus chose to suffer for me.

There is a story that Fr. Lange uses to explain how unacceptable Jesus on the cross is. There was a Franciscan who had gone off to Spain to pray and live a hermit's life. He had been there about six months when one night in prayer he saw Jesus on the cross before him. Jesus spoke to him:

Look at the nails in my hands and feet, they're for you.
Look at this crown of thorns, it's for you.
See the blood, the sweat, the dirt, it's for you.
See the wound in my side, it's for you.
When are you going to believe that I love you?

The monk jumped up and, shaking his fist, screamed at Jesus, "You're crazy to die for me. I'm not worth it." It was

51

then that he remembered something an old monk had told him early in his Franciscan life: "The day you accept that Jesus Christ died for you is the day your life will change."

And it is crazy that Jesus should die for me. We want Him to come down from the cross because we're ashamed of the way He loves us. If only he'd be sensible; dying really isn't necessary. Jesus offends us with His love. Deep down we know we wouldn't be able to believe anything less than the scandalous love of the cross.

Thomas Merton said that "the school of Christian joy is Calvary." To say that the cross was so unnecessary is to say that it was a complete gift of love. Our response is, "Alleluia! I am loved!" The passion of Jesus is His total identification with the human condition. He suffers, dies and is buried as all men must. Jesus didn't suffer more than all men, He suffered as a man. Crucifixion was a routine punishment. He even refused a noble or spectacular death. In this way Jesus becomes one with all the suffering of man. As we are betrayed, Jesus is betrayed. As we are poor, persecuted and defenseless, so is Jesus. As we must endure pain and death, Jesus does too. Our wounds are His wounds, our loneliness is His loneliness, and "by his stripes we are healed."

HE HAS RISEN

But the Good News of Jesus is that He has risen. This is simply the triumph of love over everything connected with death. This is Christ who wins for us the victory over sin (isolation) and death. We literally have nothing more to fear: "If we have died with Christ, we believe that we are also to live with him" (Romans 6:8), and because of this we are "new creations."

Jesus risen is the Lord, "seated at the right hand of the Father." *Lord* means that the defenseless Jesus now has all power in heaven and earth. He is the Lord over every other so-called god, power, prophet or ruler. What this meant to the first-century Christians was that Jesus had the strength to deliver them from any power or force. They understood this basically as deliverance from evil spirits and from the power of fate. Jesus now has the power to liberate us from any kind of fear or oppression. He is Lord over nations, poverty, destiny, death, anything which takes away our freedom. And since He is Lord, we need to give him the control of our life simply because He loves us.

Lord also means that Jesus is God and Creator. The Greek word for that is *Kyrios,* which was used to translate *Yahweh* in the Septuagint Old Testament. By saying Jesus is Kyrios the Church was witnessing that Jesus is indeed one with the Father, having the same nature as God (Phil. 2:6).

As Lord, Jesus is the New Man (New Adam), the Crown of Creation, the perfect Man. As Jesus lived and loved, so we can live and love through the power of His death and resurrection, gift of the Spirit. We now "put on Christ" and "live in Christ" and "love as Christ has loved us." This is the perfection of love, "because our life in this world is the same as Christ's" (I John 4:17). We are becoming Jesus. We are Christians, little Christs.

"God is with us" and has made human life holy. Because of the incarnation there is no more dichotomy between the natural and the supernatural. Our God worked, laughed, ate, suffered, lived and died as an ordinary man. This means that everything we do ("all things except sin") is blessed by the touch of Jesus. Anything can be a spiritual activity if it is done as Jesus did it, in union with the Father. This is what Jesus' sacrifice is all about: *(sacra —* holy, *facere —* to make) to make life holy.

This adds a whole new dimension to our Christian life. What the God-man Jesus shouts out is that creation is good, life is good, the body is good, laughter is holy, the Kingdom is a wedding feast, your God is Man, Alleluia!

Perhaps what Jesus has said with His life is too shocking and hopeful to be believed. Yet this is His message, "the foolishness of the Cross" this folly of love which is Christ, the power and the wisdom of God (I Cor. 1:24). Men will always be offended by it. If Jesus should come today, love would again be crucified. This mystery brings up the rather blunt question: What do you want to do about it?"

BIBLIOGRAPHY

RECOMMENDED READING:

Greeley, Andrew M., *The Jesus Myth: New Insights into the Person and Message of Jesus,* Image Books, Garden City, N.Y., 1973, 198pp.

Basically an explanation of what Jesus means for us and what we do about Him. No one captures the unconditional commitment and joy of the Good News better than Greeley in this amazingly enjoyable book.

SUPPLEMENTARY READING:

McKenzie, John L., *The Power and the Wisdom: An Interpretation of the New Testament,* Bruce Publishing Co., New York, N.Y., 1965, 300pp.

Excellent and clear presentation of the Gospel challenge. The first six chapters are helpful for a deeper understanding of the history and meaning of the role of Jesus.

Pope Paul VI, *Who is Jesus?,* Daughters of St. Paul, Boston, Mass., 1972, 183pp.

A collection of homilies and addresses by the Pope on the person and meaning of Jesus. I found it surprisingly good.

by Joseph Lange

How Do You Come
to Know Jesus? 4

Knowing who Jesus is and knowing *that* Jesus has been given to us as Savior brings us to the crucial question: How do we come to know Jesus? In many of our churches it has been taken for granted that we already know Jesus, which means that the business of religious education has been satisfied with talking *about* God and *about* the Church and *about* morals. The 60's saw an evasion of faith, confusion, and abandonment of prayer (cf. *Unless the Lord Build the House* by Ralph Martin). Many have even lost the sense that they *can* know God. Yet this is precisely what is at the very core of our faith. Jesus is alive; He is risen; and because He is alive, we really can know Him. He knows us and He loves us and He wants us to share our lives with Him.

In Biblical language *to know is to experience.* If we have not yet experienced the presence and power of the risen Lord, we have not yet begun to experience what Christianity is all about. Evangelicals have always known this. In Protestant or Evangelical jargon this coming to a personal knowing of Jesus is called "being saved" or "being reborn." They speak of the "saved" Christian and the "reborn" Christian.

In many Christian Churches the call to choose Jesus as Savior and Lord has been neglected. The teaching has been neglected. The teaching has been incomplete even to the point of not expecting religious experience, or, even worse, of being afraid of it. We have also suffered from both bad example and the lack of good example. Many of us have never encountered a church of people who lived daily with Jesus in a personal relationship and in expectant faith. It is especially hard to believe that it is possible to live in an intimate relationship with God when you don't know anyone who does.

There also abound a lot of fears which prevent people from wanting to know Jesus. I've heard people ask whether accepting Jesus meant that they would have to sell everything and maybe go to Africa. Just the other day I spoke with a woman who wanted to know Jesus, but was afraid to try for fear it would mean her giving up a relationship she had. There are some who fear that knowing Jesus leads to fanaticism. Others fear change or emotionalism or ridicule. Others have dreaded opening their hearts to Jesus because they know it would mean looking at themselves, and it seems as though that is more than they could bear.

Instead of attempting to deal with all the possible reasons for apprehension and misunderstanding (even if that were possible), we have found that it is more effective simply to describe how we actually do come to know Jesus and what difference that makes or can make in our lives. So let's get on with it. We have found it useful to divide the process into five steps. The division is somewhat artificial and the telling takes more time than the doing, but the method is helpful.

ACKNOWLEDGING OUR SINFULNESS

The first step consists of acknowledging our sinfulness and our sins. In our general theological perspective we have already distinguished sinfulness and sins. Because of our isolation and the influence of the world, we are not experiencing the fullness of human life that we are capable of. We have hang-ups and problems' of all kinds, fears and worries, bad relationships, weaknesses, and many potentialities that grind down or key up our feelings; or we just tolerate all sorts of things because we feel helpless to do anything about them. This is what it is to be in sin, in darkness, and perhaps it should be said emphatically again and again. Sinfulness does not mean telling lies, cheating, stealing, and all the obvious sins. We do commit sins and it is important to acknowledge them, too. But it is just as important, if not more so, to recognize the waste of human life which is our sinfulness. We were not created just to squander our lives in utter mediocrity. This is not what God has promised can be ours, what He wants for us. Life is not meant to be a rat race or the dullness of endless nights in front of a TV screen. The first step in achieving the fullness of life promised by Jesus is to acknowledge the poverty that we have settled for, to allow that our lives are not all that they might be.

ADMITTING OUR NEED FOR A SAVIOR

The second step is to acknowledge that we need a savior. That admission is not a difficult thing. If we have never said it in words to ourselves or to another, we have already lived in search of a savior, in the search for someone or something which we think would make us happy. I used to think that we human beings are really stupid. We seek satisfaction in a variety of ways, from situations, things, people; and even after we discover that these "saviors" really do not satisfy, we keep returning to them. I've changed my mind about the stupidity. Now I think that it is more a result of ignorance. Ignorance stands by itself as simply *not knowing;* but stupidity is a matter of mistaking one's ignorance for wisdom. We develop patterns in our lives for seeking solutions to our problems. For God knows how many reasons, it has never occurred to many Christians that Christ should or could be a part of those patterns. We try to find satisfaction in life, at the many levels at which we live it, apart from God. We hope that security and peace will come from money and property, the "good life," success, etc. None of them saves; none of them has ever saved; but they are our saviors, because a savior is someone or something which helps me to find the happiness, the completeness, the joy of life which I cannot seem to find by myself alone.

By ourselves we are incapable of the fullness of life. We acknowledge this every time we seek someone or something outside of ourselves. We fail to achieve the good that we would like to achieve. We need a savior. Paul puts it this way in Romans 7:14-20:

> We know that the law is spiritual, whereas I am weak flesh
> sold into the slavery of sin. I cannot even understand my
> own actions. I do not do what I want to do but what I

hate. When I act against my own will, by that very fact I agree that the law is good. This indicates that it is not I who do it but sin which resides in me. I know that no good dwells in me, that is, in my flesh; the desire to do right is there but not the power. What happens is that I do, not the good I will to do, but the evil I do not intend. But if I do what is against my will, it is not I who do it, but sin which dwells in me.

SEEING JESUS AS SAVIOR

Now, having acknowledged our sinfulness and our sins, our inability to help ourselves and our need of a savior, we come to the third step, which is acknowledging that God has given *Jesus* to us as our Savior. Paul continues in Romans 7:24: "What a wretched man I am! Who can free me from this body under the power of death? All praise to God, through Jesus Christ our Lord!" This is the good part of the Good News. This is the peace that is outside of the non-Christian (or worldly) patterns of satisfaction-seeking. It is another way, a different way. Jesus said of Himself: "I am the way, and the truth, and the life" (John 14:6).

What we are saying here is that God has made us in such a way that we are meant to live in loving communication with Himself through Jesus. What we are saying is that there is no other savior which can take the place of the one God has chosen for us. Nothing else will do. The news of the Good News is that God has not left us in the dark about this. He has told us. We now have the answer. Paul phrases it in lots of different ways:

> Praised be the God and Father of our Lord Jesus Christ, who has bestowed on us in Christ every spiritual blessing in the heavens! God chose us in him before the world began, to be holy and blameless in his sight, to be full of love; he likewise predestined us through Christ Jesus to be his adopted sons — such was his will and pleasure — that all might praise the glorious favor he has bestowed on us in his beloved.
>
> It is in Christ and through his blood that we have been redeemed and our sins forgiven, so immeasurably generous

is God's favor to us. God has given us the wisdom to understand fully the mystery, the plan he was pleased to decree in Christ, to be carried out in the fullness of time: namely, to bring all things in the heavens and on earth into one under Christ's headship.

In him we were chosen; for in the decree of God, who administers everything according to his will and counsel, we were predestined to praise his glory by being the first to hope in Christ.

(Ephesians 1:3-12)

But now the justice of God has been manifested apart from the law, even though both law and prophets bear witness to it — that justice of God which works through faith in Jesus Christ for all who believe. All men have sinned and are deprived of the glory of God. All men are now undeservedly justified by the gift of God, through the redemption wrought in Christ Jesus. Through his blood, God made him the means of expiation for all who believe. He did so to manifest his own justice, for the sake of remitting sins committed in the past — to manifest his justice in the present, by way of forbearance, so that he might be just and might justify those who believe in Jesus.

(Romans 3:21-26)

Make every effort to preserve the unity which has the Spirit as its origin and peace as its binding force. There is but one body and one Spirit, just as there is but one hope given all of you by your call.

(Ephesians 4:3, 4)

In the general theological perspective, we have been through all of this. Here we want to lay emphasis on the fact that the Good News announces that Jesus has been given to us as Savior, that fullness of life comes by accepting the Savior who is given. In his speech before the Sanhedrin, Peter said: "There is no salvation in anyone else, for there is no other name in the whole world given to men by which we are to be saved" (Acts 4:12). Peter and Paul both seem to use "faith" and "obedience" interchangeably. "Obedience" means to listen and say "yes." The point we are trying to make here is that we do not have a choice about saviors. We are asked to reject all other saviors and all other idols and accept Jesus as our only Savior and our only Lord. This is the fourth step in coming to know (experience) Jesus.

CHOOSING JESUS

Having acknowledged our sinfulness and sins, our need for a savior, and the Good News that God has given us Jesus as Savior, we find ourselves presented with a choice. Jesus stands knocking at the door of our hearts. Now we know who it is we are called upon to accept or reject. Jesus wants us to accept His love, accept Him into our lives. He wants to share Himself with us. He wants us to share our lives with Him. He wants to be the most important person in our lives. He promises that this is the way, the only way, to find real freedom, real peace, real joy, and everything else that is good in life. "Seek first his kingship over you ... and all these things will be given you besides" (Matthew 6:33). You shall love the Lord your God with your whole heart, with your whole soul, and with all your mind" (Matthew 22:37). Few things in Scripture are as clear as this. Jesus Himself is the fundamental object of choice – not dogmas or rules or styles of life. We are asked to choose for or against accepting the love of the risen Lord. He Himself was "foolishness" for the Greeks, a "stumbling block" for the Jews, and He continues to be the pivotal point of decision. Being a follower of Jesus the Christ is not a matter of birth, but of decision. This is the decision of faith. The tradition of infant baptism claims the faith of the community for the infant, but expects each individual to choose Jesus for himself when he is able to do so.

There is more to all of this, though, and this is usually where accepting Jesus sticks in some people's throats. Whatever has to do with Christianity has to do with the heart and with the ' truth. At this point we move out of the worldly understanding of religion as observances and rules to the acceptance of love. Further, the truth is that the one who offers himself and his love is the Lord. Jesus is God, which means that our relationship with Him will and must be different from our relationship with anyone else. Jesus the teacher tells us that. He came only to do His Father's will. He also tells us that when we pray we should first acknowledge God's holiness and then profess, "Thy will be done." The secret of Mary's life is in her profession: "Let it be done to me as you say." The secret of life, Jesus tells us, is to discover the will of God and do it. Jesus says to each of us: "Follow me." To follow is not to lead; it is not to do our own thing, but His thing. This is the crux of the matter, this is the great stumbling block.

We dearly love our own way. We want to be the lord of our own lives. We want to feel that we are in control. We want to decide for ourselves what is good and bad for ourselves, where we shall go, who shall be our friends, what work we shall do, and on and on even to the smallest aspects of our lives. The most frustrating part of wanting to be the lord of our lives is that our lives include others, in our family, at work, socially; and each one wants the other to be and to behave as he determines. Each wants to be the master of the other, and while he does not like to think of it that way, each wants the other to be his alone. If ever we get our back up and bristle all over, it is when we feel we are being told to do something. Rebelliousness is rooted in our determination to be self-sufficient lords. This, as we have said before, is the reason the world has developed law: to regulate the way in which self-sufficient lords may interact in peace.

FOLLOWING JESUS

Into this picture come the heralds of the Gospel of Jesus. They say that God has reconciled us to Himself in Jesus and that Jesus says to each of us: "I love you; follow me." They call us to accept Jesus as our only Savior and our only Lord. If we have really understood this, then we know that we are being called to give up our own way and accept the will of God as our Way. This involves all that we have talked about before: admitting to ourselves that we really can't make it on our own, that our way really does not work, that we need a Savior, and that God has given us a Savior in Jesus.

This is very clearly a Gospel for those who are hungry and

thirsty for a better way. It is the Gospel for the poor, the sinner, the failure, the restless. It is the Gospel for the honest seeker. The Gospel of Jesus is not for the self-sufficient, the complacent. Mary said it in her *Magnificat:* "The hungry he has given every good thing, while the rich he has sent empty away" (Luke 1:53). The sufficiency and complacency are really illusions which are maintained only with great difficulty. On the other hand, the one who has sinned and the one who is needy are often enough ready to hear the Good News that there is a way out. The way is to be a disciple of Jesus. The cost of discipleship is to accept His will, His Lordship of our lives.

EVEN UNTO DEATH

It is important for us to be very explicit and very thorough about this, because the power of God's love for us only reaches us in the full truth of our surrender to His Lordship. Jesus spoke of it in the strongest terms. He said that we must die to ourselves if we wish to follow Him. He said that he who loves life will lose it, but he that loses his life for Jesus' sake will find it. He gave us the image of the seed: unless the seed falls into the ground and dies, it cannot bear fruit. What all this means is that we must die to our self-centeredness, our selfishness, our desire to control our own lives, and seek His will for us. This "dying" is giving up our way by choosing to follow His way. We have to give up our will to act independently of what God wants. We have to give up our isolation and listen to what God wants for us in Jesus.

Dying is not something we want to do naturally. In an extremely powerful and interesting book, *On Death and Dying,* Elizabeth Keibler-Ross describes her research on the reactions of people who have been told they are going to die. She discovered that such people almost invariably go through the same pattern. The first reaction is one of disbelief, manifested by such things as ignoring the diagnosis or seeking the opinion of another doctor. The second stage is anger, the kind that is without any particular object and so is liable to fall on anyone or anything. At this stage the person may be angry at God, the doctor, his family, hospital personnel — for no apparent reason. It's a reaction to the "Why me? Why not someone else?" There is a sense of the inevitability of the diagnosis, and this is a reaction against it. There is a sense that this is beyond my control.

The next stage is compromise, which is manifested by attempts at bargaining for a little more time. "OK, God, but give me just a few more months and I'll do this and that for you."

When the realization occurs that none of this works, depression follows. It is a time of recognizing the inescapable and of feeling that I am losing everything.

Finally comes acceptance, and with acceptance comes peace.

Now, Scripture has always connected sin and death. Father James Finnegan, OSFS, has suggested a parallel here between the way we react to the call for dying to sin and dying to our earthly existence. I think it is really helpful to recognize these stages in ourselves and others. It gives us a measure of control over them. It helps us to understand ourselves and others better.

Jesus says that you must love the Lord your God with your whole heart, your whole soul, your whole strength, and your whole mind and you must love your neighbor as yourself. He says seek *first* the Kingdom of Heaven. He says that He alone is Savior and Lord. He asks you to die to your own desires and your own will. What is your reaction? The Jews replied: "We have Abraham for our Father, we don't need you." The Greeks grumbled: "This is foolishness." The complacent answer: "We can make it on our own." The "religious" man retorts: "I go to church and lead a good life. I follow the laws. I don't need any of this talk." Is it not true that when we hear that challenge, that clear, naked challenge, we want to say: "Not me. That's OK for the clergy and for people who have time for it, but I don't need it." The first reaction is one of disbelief. Or, perhaps we have already tried to follow the Lord, and now we become aware that we really have not let Jesus be the Lord of a particular relationship. Are we not inclined to say: "Not that, too!" The answer to people in this frame of mind is simply: "Yes, this is what Jesus wants."

Then comes anger. "I'm not going back to those religious fanatics anymore." "Who does that priest think he is, saying that to me? The whole Church is phony." "Who could possibly live that way?" Again and again I've seen people go through this nameless anger. I've gone through it myself. There is a clear sense that a sensitive area has been hit on the head, and we don't like it at all. Dealing with ourselves and others at this stage is a matter of patience. Sooner or later we get through it.

Then there is often a compromise stage. Again, the truth is facing us and its inevitability is clear enough. We would like to put if off for a while, though. The classic example is St. Augustine's prayer: "Lord, make me pure, but not yet." I know a person who knew clearly that she had to break off a bad relationship. Instead she tried doubling her prayer time and doing all kinds of good works. It did not do the trick.

Next comes depression. This is really important because it is so often overlooked. A lot of people who are seeking Christ go through depression of sorts. One man I know had turned over his life to Jesus and found a great peace and a quiet joy that lasted for almost six months. Then he got depressed. We didn't see him around for a while. He was angry with us and angry with life. He could not figure out why until he realized that he had been resisting giving up his own way about an aspect of his life. When he accepted it, the depression left.

So, finally, comes acceptance. Thy will be done. This is the only final answer to depression of this sort. It means accepting the Lordship of Jesus.

FULLER LIFE

We should not be surprised at ourselves for being resistant and rebellious, nor should we be surprised that it happens to others. But now, at least, we ought to be able to understand what is happening to us and how to deal with it. The answer, the only answer, is to surrender. Of course, we may feel that we are giving up something that is really good. We may feel very insecure in yielding control over our lives. But connected with the call to die is the promise that a new life will come to us, a life that is richer and fuller than anything we had ever hoped for. This is what we believe. This is what supports us. We believe that God is faithful to His promises.

Incidentally, one significant difference between facing

physical death and the call to die to our self-sufficiency is that physically we die only once, but following Jesus means dying over and over again. We don't get any practice or any experience with physical death, but dying to ourselves can become a way of life. And the more we yield to God's call to let go of our own way and follow Him, the more experience we get in the rewards of doing so. It is not long before we accumulate enough experience of the new life, which comes through giving up the lordship of our lives to Jesus, that we begin to welcome the awareness of new challenges to let go. After a while we begin to skip the various stages and yield immediately. We become eager to let Jesus show us the way.

I can still vividly recall my efforts to mobilize a college campus for Christ. I pressured people, studied, argued, cajoled, persuaded, and got angry. I schemed and organized and in general was rather obnoxious. And then one day it occurred to me that *I* was trying to build the Church there without ever asking the Lord how *He* wanted it done. I had spent a great deal of time and energy doing my thing, and it was not working. So I turned the work and my life over to the Lord again (I had done this lots of times before — don't we all?), and He led me to a totally different apostolate that is bearing fruit in His way. The peace and the joy of that decision has been with me for over three years — except when I try to take control again. Turning your life over to the Lord really works.

Now, having said all of that, dotting our "i's" and crossing our "t's", let us simplify it. It all comes down to a simple prayer from the heart:

Jesus, I don't like the way I am.

I've tried to live independently of you.

I've tried to run my own life and I just haven't succeeded.

I'm not very loving; I'm not very peaceful;

I'm not at all the kind of person I would really like to be.

I'm sorry that I've left you out of my life.

I'm sorry that I have hurt so many people

and failed so many others — including myself.

I don't want to be that way anymore.

I ask you to forgive me and heal me.

65

I need you and I want to share my life with you.
Jesus, I accept you as my Lord and my Savior.
Come into my heart and share your life with me.
I want you to be the most important person in my life.
Jesus, show me your face that I might love you.
Let me experience your presence and your power in my life.

THE SACRAMENT OF RECONCILIATION

A prayer like that is one way of beginning or renewing your relationship with Jesus. Another way is the Sacrament of Reconciliation, the Sacrament of Penance. This particular sacrament is Jesus' way of being present to us as the One who forgives and the One who heals. There are lots of things we could say about this sacrament, but here we want to focus on how to use it effectively, how to use it as an effective means of reconciliation.

The first ingredient for a good confession is an attitude, a way of approaching Jesus. We come to Jesus, not as though we are advancing toward a washing machine, but as people who hope to reestablish a relationship. If we attempt to put the attitude into words, it comes out something like the prayer above. We come to Jesus to ask forgiveness and healing because we really want to start over with Him. Confession, then, like prayer, becomes *part of a way of life,* and not just an isolated experience. It implies a desire to build the relationship after our reconciliation.

It also means that confession is not just a matter of reciting a list of "sins." It is an encounter with the one whom we have offended or neglected, and we come to the encounter wanting to be reconciled. So we've got to be honest. We've got to clear the air. We've got to look at our basic sinfulness as well as our sins and look at them as honestly as we can, not covering over anything, not finding nice ways to say it. Call a spade a spade. Putting your sinfulness and your sins into words is an important part of declaring your desire for reconciliation. We all know how important it is to apologize, both for ourselves and for the other. The same is true here. And, again, tell it like it is. Instead of "I had bad thoughts," which is a bit childish, say, "I am guilty of lust." Instead of "I took some things from work," say, "I stole. . . ." The point is that you are coming to meet Jesus and you want to start over. You want to be really forgiven and really healed. So speak the truth clearly and without games or softening words. Get it all out in the open the way you really feel it, and give the Lord a chance to take it away.

Coming to meet Jesus in this sacrament is possible because He is alive. We can come to Him in the same way that His contemporaries did two thousand years ago in Palestine. We can come with an expectant faith asking not only to be forgiven of our sins, but healed of our guilt, the effects of sin in our lives, the root of sin in our lives. Each of us shares in the Spirit of God. Ask the Spirit to bring to your mind what you should confess, what the roots of your sins are. After confessing your sins and the source of them, ask Jesus to heal you, so that you will not fall again. It is our expectant faith that releases the power of the Spirit in our lives. Expect the Spirit to enlighten you and heal you and He will.*

Many priests today are "hearing" confessions with a new faith in the power of the Holy Spirit, with a new expectancy that the Spirit has been given us to change our lives. Many of them pray with the penitent for the gifts of knowledge or wisdom or discernment in order to discover the source of sin and sinfulness and in order to know what to do about it. They also pray for healing of sinfulness and the sense of guilt. I've done it myself as a regular thing for the past two years, and again and again the Lord has been faithful to His promise. People are being forgiven and healed. The Lord does care. He does not want us to remain in our weakness. He wants us to expect that we can be healed.

It should be added here, too, that the Sacrament of Reconciliation is the most appropriate and most effective way of being reconciled to God. If we go to Jesus in private and seek His forgiveness, there is no doubt that we have it. The sacrament, on the other hand, is not only the Lord's way of

---

*Father Michael Scanlon, T.O.R., has written a powerful booklet on this: *The Power in Penance*, Ave Maria Press, Notre Dame, 1972. It's the best book I know for preparing for Penance.

being present in a special way for us, it is an ecclesial act, the act of the Body of Christ; and it is the Body of Christ which is empowered to forgive sin. The sacramental encounter through the confessing to a priest is an encounter with the Body of Christ in the person of its appointed representative. If we know what we are doing, then we are reminded in this way that our guilt and our weakness and the effects of our sinfulness are not just between God and ourselves but are connected with the life of the Body. When I sin, I infect the whole Body with my sinfulness. Because I sin, I scandalize others. Because I fail to love, the Body is experienced as unloving. Because I fail to nourish my relationship with Jesus in prayer, the faith and love and spirituality of the whole Body suffers.

Let it be said once and for all: confession to Jesus alone is simply not enough. When we sin we fail our brothers and sisters as well. We need to confess to them, too. In confession we speak to their representative, the appointed representative of the Body of Christ. He forgives in the name of Jesus and in the name of the Body of Christ. Our righteousness before God is not complete unless we have Christ. Our righteousness before God is not complete unless we have also established a right relationship with our neighbor. Confessing to a representative of our brothers and sisters is one aspect of being in a right relationship with our neighbor. We'll get to other aspects in later chapters.

Finally, let us remember what this whole chapter is about: coming to know Jesus by accepting Him as our Savior and Lord. He loves us and He really wants to share His life with us. Jesus is the answer, the Way, the Truth, and the Life. So once we have acknowledged our sinfulness, let us move on to look at Jesus who forgives us. Contrition usually ends by our wallowing in guilt, perhaps with tears. Christian repentance never stops there. The repentant Christian stops looking at himself and looks at the God who is so good, who forgives and heals. Once the Christian acknowledges his sin and asks forgiveness, he sings, "Glory to God in the highest." The key to the new life is that we leave the old life behind and now look at *God,* at who He is and how good He is; and we look to God for guidance and healing.

BIBLIOGRAPHY

RECOMMENDED READING:

Scanlon, Michael, T.O.R., *The Power in Penance,* Ave Maria Press, Notre Dame, Indiana, 1972, 62pp.
   How to use the Sacrament of Confession in order to make it a positive, transforming encounter with the person of Jesus.

Schlink, Basilea, *Realities,* Zondervan, Grand Rapids, Michigan, 1966, 128pp.
   The astounding story of faith, love and answered prayers in the founding of the Lutheran Sisterhood of Mary.

Schlink, Basilea, *Repentance — the Joy-filled Life,* Zondervan, Grand Rapids, Michigan, 1968, 61pp.
   Brutally practical since it's based on personal experience of the positive choice of Jesus. Christian repentance is not all guilt and sorrow; it is honest love and joy.

Miller, Keith, *A Taste of New Wine,* Word Books, Waco, Texas, 1965, 116pp.
   Easy reading story of how one man met and fell in love with Jesus.

SUGGESTED READING:

   As background for this chapter, you can pick up any one of literally hundreds of personal witness stories, from The Confessions of St. Augustine *to* Run, Baby, Run *by Nicki Cruz.*

by Tony Cushing

Personal Prayer: Being Friends with God 5

Prayer is a difficult and yet very wonderful topic for me to talk about. It is difficult because I know my many failures in prayer. It is wonderful because over the last three years of attempting to pray, I've come to experience the tremendous love that Jesus has for me and to glimpse a little of how much He wants to comfort, heal and change me.

To put it simply, talking with Jesus makes me happy. However, I'm stupid enough to forget that, and so I've stopped talking to Him at times. Gradually, the experience of how dead life is when I stop praying has helped me to become wiser. And because of the experience of how prayer has changed my life, I'm convinced that it's absolutely necessary to pray every day, every minute if possible.

I didn't always believe this (much less try to practice it). So I have a lot of mistakes to share with you. That helps in itself, because on this pilgrimage with Jesus it's good to know where the popular wrong turns are. Many people tried to warn me of these wrong turns. They told me constantly, *"The most important decision of your Christian life is to commit yourself to a regular time of prayer every day."* I didn't believe them. So I learned the hard way. This is what you call the "hard knocks" school of prayer. It's very effective but very unnecessary.

So, what I want to do first is describe a few essentials of prayer that apply to all Christians. Also, I want to share my own experience of prayer and the experience of my community as a witness to "Taste and see how good the Lord is" (Psalm 34:9). In doing this I want to stress the common sense dynamics of building a loving relationship.

71

LOVING GOD

You shall love the Lord your God
with your whole heart,
with your whole soul,
and with all your mind.

This is the greatest and first commandment.

(Matthew 22:37, 38)

What does this mean? How can we love God in this way? How can Jesus command this love? Isn't He just exaggerating to make a point?

To begin answering these questions — Jesus seems to be commanding us to love God as a person. We are to love God for Himself because we know who He is. God is to be, without rival, *the most important person in our life.* This applies to everyone who wants to follow Jesus, whether working man, monk, housewife or preacher — all of us are to love God as No. 1, with everything we've got.

Now, imagine you met a man who said he loved this girl with all his heart, mind, etc. Imagine you started asking questions about his relationship and you got answers like:

"Well, I love her and all that, but I really don't enjoy talking to her too much. As a matter of fact, I fall asleep a lot when I'm with her, so sometimes I don't see her for a week or even more. But I do talk to her once in a while. I ask her for a lot of things I need, but I usually don't have the time to listen to her and my mind wanders a lot, you know.

"Well, she writes these beautiful letters but, again, I just don't have the time to read them.

"We do go to a big party every Sunday, but even then, with all the other people around, I just don't have time to be alone with her. But I really love her; believe me, I do."

After talking with this character for a while I'm sure we would find his method of loving incredible. After all, almost everyone knows that if you want love to work, you've got to spend time at it. That the man refused to share his life, his time, with the person he claimed to love would lead me to say that he really didn't love her that much.

72

But are we Christians any better with the one we claim to love with our whole heart, mind and soul? How much we ignore our lover! Why do we do this? How can we change this?

MISCONCEPTIONS ABOUT PRAYER

Many people want to pray. Most of us have a lot of difficulty doing it. Lots more have even given up trying. One of the reasons for this exodus from prayer is that we have many misconceptions about what prayer is. The first falsehood is that prayer really isn't that important. It isn't something real people are supposed to be concerned with. Somehow the idea got around that prayer is for monks and invalids or anyone else who has nothing worthwhile to do. "After all, people in the real world don't have the time for all of that. All you really have to do is try to be good. Prayer is extra credit." Many people equate prayer with fire alarms — something to be used only in emergencies. This makes Jesus some kind of bellhop in-the sky who only comes to mind when we need room service. Yet, Jesus calls us His friends because everything He has, He has given to us. What kind of friends are we to Jesus who has given His life for us? How would you like a friend who only talked to you when he needed something from you? As with the man who didn't have time to talk to his beloved, you would be skeptical of the Christian who found it impossible to talk to his lover, Jesus.

The first way out of this dilemma is to realize that our whole life is concerned with building a loving relationship with God. We are to love God with everything we've got. That means that prayer is the most important thing I do. Everything else — work, family, friends, recreation — is secondary to sharing my life with God in prayer. This is *not* just for monks; all Christians are called to be holy by joining their life with God. St. Francis of Assisi said that "... those to whom the Lord has given the ability to work shall work faithfully and devotedly in such wise that ... they do not quench the *spirit of holy prayer* and devotion, *to which all other temporal activities must be subordinate.*"

This makes a lot of sense, especially if you think of where you're coming from and where you're going. The answer here is life with God. The goal of our whole lives is heaven: to be totally united in love with God. Everything else will pass away. Everything! At the end God will be all and in all (1 Cor. 15:28). Heaven comes to earth when we are in love with God. And this means that prayer is essential for everyone.

OK, if we accept that prayer is necessary, then what do we mean by prayer? There are plenty of misconceptions here also. There's a certain attitude that "all my life is a prayer. My work is prayer. I offer my whole day to God every morning; that's my prayer." And it's very possible your life *can be prayer.* However, it doesn't have to be prayer. Your life can be prayer if everything you do is done in union with Jesus, in His presence, loving Him. And some people after years of building a friendship with Jesus are so close to Him that they work with Him and eat and sleep and party with Him. This is the goal of the relationship, not the beginning. Just think of the common understanding of a personal relationship. You wouldn't believe that two teenagers who've dated a few times are so close that everything they do, they do together. You might believe it of a couple who've been married thirty years. It's the same with Jesus. All of us are to be married to God; then our life can be prayer.

SPENDING TIME WITH GOD

How do we build this marriage with God? Well, how do you build any other relationship? You spend time with a person to get to know him. This is a very natural thing to do.

When a man and a woman start to think of marriage, they spend lots of time together just talking. And they do this in a committed and structured way. Imagine two people who really like each other and want to get to know each other better. One says to the other, "I think I could fall in love with you. Even this little time together has been important to me. Next time I happen to bump into you, we'll chat." No, they make a date. Building the relationship is important enough to set aside a certain time to share. And it's only if a great emergency happens

74

that they break the date. Otherwise, the person is "stood up" — an insult that breaks off the relationship.

Now, as two people spend more and more time sharing, they begin to trust one another. As they share both the good and the bad sides of their life, they *experience* the faithfulness of the other person's love. You gradually find out that the other person loves you "for better and for worse, through thick and thin." You know and trust that the other person accepts you. At this. point, even sane people will want to get married. They have faith in one another. And this belief is not just a wild leap into the dark. It's based on communication and the experience of being loved for who you are.

What I'm trying to do is to make a Big Point. Our relationship with God has the same dynamics as a marriage relationship. As we spend more and more time getting to know Him, we can have faith in His love. The *experience* of the faithfulness of Jesus' love is the only sensible reason to commit our whole lives to Him, to marry Him — in a way that is more complete than any earthly marriage.

This means making dates with Jesus. Structuring our time so that we can spend time alone with Him. This has to do with the everyday realities of our life — what to do with our time. Organizing our time so that we can be in union with God is the very first and most basic way we can repent or give our life to Him. Most of the people we've encountered have difficulty praying simply because they never take the time. They leave it up to chance: they'll pray when they feel like it. For all the people who've tried this (myself included), I don't know of one who succeeded.

The nitty-gritty of this is to *schedule a certain time every day* to be alone with Jesus. We have to *make time* to pray. This proves that we think it's important to pray. So we take a block of time and make it sacred. That time is for Jesus; everything else stops. This is to say that as we grow, some things get more valuable and other things get less valuable. Prayer becomes more valuable than watching TV, chatting with a crony or even keeping the house immaculately clean. Millions of Christians who schedule a whole night a week for bowling might think it excessive to schedule an hour a day for the God who loves them.

This might also mean that you have to stop doing some things you're used to doing, so that you can pray. And it involves real effort and discipline. If you think that love doesn't mean work and discipline, just ask a married couple of 25 years or so. It is not simply a matter of spontaneity or good feelings. In a relationship with someone, to remain on the level of the spontaneous is to condemn yourself to the superficial.

I say this very confidently as if it were always obvious to me. Well, it took me about a year even to schedule a time for prayer. For me to organize something just wasn't "natural" enough. It wasn't romantic or exciting. Schedules were bourgeois. The result was that I found myself forgetting to pray for days on end. And the less I'd pray, the more difficult it became to be loving. Eventually, the joy of Jesus would melt away until something big happened. Then I'd repent and try to remember to pray. But it just didn't work. I wanted to pray; I even liked praying; but I never found time for it. It finally dawned on me that I couldn't trust myself to pray just because I felt like it. So I finally "heard" what more experienced Christians had been telling me and decided that every day from three to four I would talk to Jesus. I had to make a habit of prayer. Nothing else worked.

The same kind of thing happened to most of the people in our prayer community. One friend of mine worked ten hours a day and spent most of his evening hours at meetings. The only time he had to pray was his lunch hour. So he ate lunch in ten minutes and prayed for fifty minutes. I know housewives who make agreements to take care of each others' children so that they can have time to pray. Recently, I made an agreement with a friend that we call each other every day just as a reminder to pray. The most impressive witness was about two years ago when the whole group had gone through a very trying summer and had lost about half its members. Fr. Lange got up and asked why the rest of us were still around. One after another, the whole group said that they had all been fed up with community at one time or another but that they realized it happened at the times when they had stopped praying. As soon as they returned to prayer, a lot of the dissatisfaction disappeared. Unaminously we accepted the fact that personal prayer was the basis of our life together.

A TIME, A PLACE

What we have understood from this experience is that everyone should have a regular time of private prayer of at least a half hour every day. Half an hour is not an arbitrary choice — it takes at least that long to relax and clear our minds of all the events of the day. Many people are discouraged in prayer simply because they don't take enough time. Again, if we look at our everyday friendships, we'd never expect to have a meaningful discussion in ten or fifteen minutes. It takes a while to get past the superficialities into intimate dialogue. It's only after years of close sharing that we can be immediately honest and open with an old friend. Unless we're intensely intimate with Jesus, it will take us some time to be present to Him.

We also discovered that it matters *when* you pray. Somehow our idea of prayer and common sense can get separated. Scheduling prayer for 6:00 AM and being surprised that you keep falling asleep brings little credit to your I.Q. The same thing happens if you choose the time right before bed — you end up meditating the pillow. Now, some people are most alert at 6:00 AM, some at 11:00 PM. If possible, schedule your prayer for the time when you are most alert. It's a matter of common sense.

We have also discovered that it's helpful to have a regular *place* to pray. It might seem too obvious to mention, but it should be a place where you can be alone and free from distractions. If you wanted to have a serious discussion with a friend, you wouldn't choose a crowded bus to talk. Of course, it's possible, but it isn't preferable. Well, what happens if you feel like singing to God and people keep dropping in on you? The result is that you keep one eye over your shoulder expecting to be interrupted and get very inhibited. A regular place to pray also conditions us to a habit of prayer. If you have one definite place to pray, as soon as you get there you expect to pray. It's like every time a housewife goes into the kitchen, she expects to do something about meals. Bishop McKinney of Grand Rapids has a prayer chair. Every time he sits in it, he almost automatically prays.

What I'm trying to convey is the value of ritual in our daily life. I used to think of ritual with a negative connotation of meaningless, sterile externals. Rituals kept you from being real or being yourself. It took a delightful book, *The Little Prince* by Antoine de St. Exupery, to make me see that ritual can help you to be yourself.

The Little Prince meets a fox and wants to be friends with him. The fox says that he has to be tamed first. He explains to the Little Prince that he should come and sit with him every day and get a little closer each day and after a while they will trust each other.

One day the Little Prince is late and the fox is disappointed. "You must come every day at the same time. Otherwise I'll never know when to expect you. If you come at four o'clock, then at three o'clock I will start to get my heart ready to greet you. If you come at anytime, I won't have my heart prepared in happiness." He added that this is a ritual "which makes one day different from the next" and it makes you free to enjoy things. Ritual builds expectations and prepares us for an encounter.

We need to have Jesus "tame us" so that we can be His friend. If we come to Him every day at the same time, then we can "prepare our hearts to greet him." This gives us an oasis of love during the day. We can prepare and expect to have this time to enjoy loving God.

SIMPLE AND SINCERE

If I haven't talked too much about what happens in prayer, it's because without these practical fundamentals, nothing will happen.

How do I pray? What do I pray?

> The Spirit too helps us in our weakness, for we do not know how to pray as we ought; but the Spirit himself makes intercession for us with groanings which cannot be expressed in speech.

> (Romans 8:26)

Christian prayer is first of all a matter of the work of the Holy Spirit. We can experience God, know God, even talk to Him only through the power of the Holy Spirit. Prayer is pleading for the Spirit to come to inspire us and "fill us with the fire of divine love."

The best way of praying is to be *simple, honest* and *spontaneous.* You are communicating with the person who knows you and loves you totally. So, be yourself. Talk to God as a brother and friend. "A man has faith when he speaks to God as one does to a man" (Cure of Ars). I don't know why we ever thought we had to be formal with God, our friend. What would it be like if a man came home and described his day to his wife in King James English? It wouldn't be respectful, just hysterical.

Talking to God is telling Him what we feel like, sharing what's important to us. If anything good happened, share it with Him and rejoice. If you're depressed or angry, tell Him and ask for help. We don't have to worry how we express ourselves. He's the one person who will always understand.

This simplicity of talking to God as a person came very early to me. The reason for this was that I had never tried formal prayer in my life except for great emergencies. The first time I really talked to Jesus was when I first experienced His love. I felt He was my friend, so I talked to Him that way. Jesus was my buddy. He knew me. So, as I'd go through a day, I'd just say, "Hey, Jesus, did you see that?" or "Boy, I feel great, Jesus. Thanks for smiles." It was fun talking to Him.

To pray is to encounter and communicate with the person of Jesus. It is building a friendship. What matters is the quality of the conversation, not the quantity or style. Ten long, boring conversations with someone probably won't make a friendship. But, if we honestly open up with someone in sharing who we are, chances are real friendship and intimacy can evolve. We get interested in the other person and want to talk with him. The way we get interested in Jesus is that, in honestly talking with Him, we experience the way He loves us. To accept this love is to have our hearts of stone changed to hearts of flesh (Ezechiel 36:26) so that we want to be with Jesus.

TALKING WITH JESUS

What I find really helpful is to imagine the physical presence of Jesus. To talk to God as you would talk to a human friend is to talk to the man-God Jesus. If I sit down to pray, Jesus is sitting in the other chair and I just talk with Him. I think of what He might be doing — smiling, putting an arm around me to comfort me, or, if I sing, maybe He starts dancing. Sometimes I think of the things He did on earth and imagine what it would have been like to be there with Him. So I can talk with Him on the road to Emmaus or at the wedding feast at Cana. Most of all I talk to Him as He was dying on the cross. As a man, Jesus laughed, prayed, got frustrated, was tempted and suffered. He knows what it's like to be human. If we find it hard to do the Father's will, then we have Jesus in the garden. If we had a wonderful day, we have Jesus rejoicing in the Holy Spirit. One time last spring I was outside praying and getting intoxicated with the beauty of creation. To be blunt, I had spring fever. I tried to fight this "distraction" until I got fed up and asked, "Jesus, did you ever get spring fever?" Immediately, I had this picture of Jesus walking around the sea of Galilee — enjoying life, then lying down on a hillside to talk to and enjoy His Father. Even my spring fever was something that Jesus wanted to share with me.

Much of what I'm talking about has been traditionally described as "living in the presence of God." We don't live this way naturally; we have to *enter into* the presence of God. There is nothing magical about this. We enter into the presence of God in the same way we are present to anyone else in a conversation. Have you ever had a conversation with someone when you knew he wasn't listening? He didn't respond to what you were saying but only talked about what he wanted to say. Think of the times you were that way — preoccupied with problems, bored, thinking about anything but the person in front of you. Now, to be present to someone is to focus your attention on him. You forget about what you want to say, forget past problems or future worries and become absorbed in what he's saying. When two people do this they are having a dialogue. They spontaneously share, listen and respond in an effortless way.

When we *focus our attention on Jesus,* we can dialogue with Him. We are present to Him. Doing this opens us up to the power of the Holy Spirit so that we can experience the joy of God's presence.

Christian prayer is turning toward another person: Jesus. If it becomes simply introspection or internal conversation, it dies. So many people find prayer boring because their prayer is self-centered, not Jesus-centered. We are always bored with ourselves. After all, we've heard it all before.

Jesus-centered prayer requires that we free ourselves from distractions so that we can turn to Him. If you don't know how to do this with your friends, you'll probably find it difficult to do in prayer. It means literally: Stop thinking about the problems of the day and start thinking about Jesus. Taking enough time and finding a quiet place are prerequisites. Using your imagination to picture Jesus helps a lot. After all, we are usually distracted by our fantasies in prayer. So instead of shutting off your imagination, use it to direct you to God.

SINGING

There are a number of other things that help me to break the stream of self-preoccupation and to focus on Jesus. The first is *singing.* Augustine says that "he who sings prays twice." The Jews had a concept of what it is to say, "Awake, my soul." They would sing the psalms to make themselves sensitive to God's presence. They were preparing to encounter God. If you put your whole heart and soul into a song to Jesus, you forget about everything else. When I lift up my arms in praise and sing, "Alleluia! Praise God in His holy dwelling" (Ps. 150), I become more aware of what I am doing in beginning prayer. Singing in the prayer gift of tongues opens us up to God in the same way. Sometimes I'll sing in tongues for ten or fifteen minutes just to help me be in God's presence.

Another help is reading the psalms aloud. This doesn't necessitate meditating on them but using them as prayers of praise and thanksgiving. If you really feel them you seem to shout out,

Bless the Lord, O my soul;

and all my being, bless his holy name.
He pardons all your iniquities,
he heals all your ills.
Bless the Lord, O my soul!

(Psalm 103:1, 3, 22)

We shouldn't be afraid of vocal prayer. If we are learning to pray, speaking out loud makes our prayers more real to us. It also helps us to concentrate. This is really evident in spontaneous praising and thanking God. The more we experience how loving and good God is, the more we praise Him in love. This too is the work of the Holy Spirit. We praise Him because we know Him, and the Spirit comes and inspires us to pour out praise for our beloved.

Let me sing the canticle of love,
let me follow thee, my Beloved, on high,
let my soul lose herself in thy praises,
rejoicing exceedingly in thy love.

(Imitation of Christ III, Ch. 5)

What we do is let go of our inhibitions and praise the God who has set us free. I'll talk more about this in the chapter on charismatic prayer.

THANKSGIVING

The priest sings in the Canon of the Mass: "It always and everywhere is right to give you thanks and praise." We can thank God for everything and anything. As we realize that "Every worthwhile gift, every genuine benefit comes from above, descending from the Father of the heavenly luminaries" (James 1:17), we want to thank God. The more we experience His love in what He does for us, the more we become grateful. It really helps to remember and rejoice in what God has done for you. So much of the Psalms is giving thanks to God for saving His people. The Mass is the thanksgift for and memorial of how Jesus has saved us and is presently saving us through His death and resurrection. I know that many times when I'm feeling blah or depressed, I just start to thank God for everything He's done for me. I thank Him for the joy of first meeting Him. Thank Him for the way He changed me. Thank

Him for healing my friend of sickness. Thank Him for the gift of tongues. Thank Him for my friends. After a while I start to trust in Him again, simply because I'm aware of how much He has done for me. I start to feel very blessed in terms of how many everyday gifts Jesus has given me. "Thank you, Jesus, for that good lunch. Thank you for the way Joe smiles. Thanks, Jesus, for clouds. Thanks for the colors I see. Thanks for this car. Thank you, Lord, for dying for me in love."

This isn't something mechanical, but ultimately sincere and personal. Thank Jesus for the things that you *are* grateful for. Again, the simpler and more spontaneous, the better. The more direct and personal our prayer becomes, the more the Spirit comes to help us. The reason for this is that the Spirit works in real people, not in the masks we often wear.

Part of being real with Jesus is expressing with our bodies what we feel inside. If you feel like praising God, stand up and lift up your arms to Him. If you're humbled by how great He is, kneel. Sometimes, if you're experiencing a profound unworthiness, prostrate yourself before the Lord of heaven and earth. But if you're bored, don't lie down, or all you'll express is sleep. Common sense will tell you that beds and easy chairs are more conducive to drowsiness than to attentiveness. Just watch two friends having an interesting discussion. You can see their attentiveness in their bodies. It's the same when you're talking to Jesus.

TECHNIQUES

Sometimes it helps to practice a certain technique or method of prayer to help us to be present to God. A very old and generally useful method is the Jesus Prayer. It is commonplace among Eastern Christian monks. For them it's the heart of their prayer life. Basically, this form of prayer means keeping the name of Jesus on your lips and in your mind all day. Usually it's the words, "Lord Jesus Christ, Son of God, have mercy on me, a sinner." Right now I don't want to talk about using this as a perpetual prayer but only as a form of vocal prayer.

What I usually do is to try to quiet myself and just speak the name of Jesus very slowly every time I exhale. As I relax and clear my mind, I add little praises or ejaculations. "Jesus, You are my Lord. Jesus, You are so good. Jesus, You are really faithful. Jesus, You are the light. Jesus, You are joy."

The Church has always taught that we should "praise the name of the Lord" and that there is a real power in the name *Jesus.* This comes from the Hebrew tradition that the name was considered a substitute for the person. That is why to know the name of Yahweh was to experience His power and reality. This is perfected in Jesus. We have faith in His name (John 3:18), preach in His name (Acts 5:40), work miracles (Mark 16:7), and are forgiven (Acts 10:43) in His name, which is above every other name (Phil. 2:9-11). The life and prayer of the Church is in the name of our Lord and Savior Jesus Christ, for He is present when two or three are gathered in His name (Matt. 18:20). Even to say in faith that "Jesus is Lord" requires an impulse of the Holy Spirit (1 Cor. 12:3).

As we breathe the name of Jesus, we are more aware of the Spirit who is the breath and life of God. This is not magic; it has to do with being in love. Think of how two lovers use each other's name especially when they are making love. It's really all that's necessary. Sometimes I'll pray the Jesus Prayer for an hour. This is usually when I'm worried or angry. It's all I can do to call on His name, but He soon restores peace.

As our prayer becomes more personal and spontaneous, our old rote prayers start to have a deeper meaning. You start to experience what *Our Father* means because you know Him as a father: "by the Spirit's power we cry to God, Father, my Father!" (Romans 8:15 — TEV). We experience that the coming of His Kingdom is what's going to make us happy. The same thing happens with the prayers of the Mass. The *Gloria* has become one of my favorite prayers because it describes my experience of God. I was bored with the rosary until I "discovered" that it was meditating on the life of Jesus.

There is another purpose for rote prayers which has more to do with perseverance. Sometimes we're too faithless, weak or even too sick to talk to Jesus, so we pray as best we can manage. Rote prayers come in handy at these times. I can remember praying the Our Father for hours, just trying to believe what I was saying.

I have mentioned all of these things in the way of helpful hints. Singing, praying the Psalms, praise and thanksgiving, the Jesus Prayer, rote prayers are all part of what prayer is. And, depending on what kind of person you are, these might take on greater or lesser meaning from time to time. What I want to stress is that any way of prayer *which brings you close to God* is best for you. There is no right method of prayer for everyone. Whatever is the simplest, even easiest form is what usually works in experiencing the love of Jesus.

I say this because I've experienced something of what forced methods of prayer can do. About three years ago I started reading about the mystical life. I quickly decided to plunge myself into meditation and mortification so that I could waltz into the contemplative life. The result was chaos and a complete loss of peace and joy. Many others have also gotten carried away on technique. It's like being so concerned about having the proper style of dancing that you never have a good time at a party. Different methods do help, but we have to remember Brother Lawrence's advice that prayer is simply "to be in the presence of God through love."

So the bulk of prayer is freely conversing with Jesus to build a friendship with Him. We get to know Him. Prayer is where we learn how much of a lover Jesus is, how forgiving He is, how faithful and compassionate. And as we daily experience His love, we can trust Him more and more. As this happens, Jesus transforms our very person. He heals us of anxiety, insecurity, guilt and inferiority. As we trust Him with more and more of our lives, this peace and joy floods our lives. "I have said these things to you so that my joy might be in you and your joy might be complete" (John 15:11).

PRAYING TO BE CHANGED

Much of this inner healing has to do with praying for ourselves in faith. We all have problems — personality conflicts, wrong behavior, character defects. Usually these come out in disturbances in our personal relationships. We can't get along with someone — "She's too proud." "That guy just never listens to me." "He's always so dominating." We have found that most of us blame the other person for problems in a relationship. Naturally, if you think that way when you pray about the situation, you'll be saying, "Lord, change him, make him more loving." I used to pray this way, and I discovered that it doesn't work. Jesus just doesn't want to hear it.

The solution, as Keith Miller points out in *A Second Touch,* is to *pray for yourself to change.* We are usually part of the problem, if not all of it. As Jesus said, "How can you say to your brother, 'Let me take that speck out of your eye,' while all the time the plank remains in your own? Hyprocrite! Remove the plank from your own eye first; then you will see clearly to take the speck from your brother's eye" (Matt. 7:4, 5). Most of the time this entails asking Jesus to take away the bitterness and grudges we might have against someone. It always involves our forgiving someone and forgetting the hurt he caused. Then the Lord can help us take the plank out of our own eye. He can heal our fear of revealing ourself, fear of being dominated, fear that we're stupid or ugly. Any kind of barrier to love He can take away.

A friend of mine, after graduating from college, returned home to live with his parents, and it was agony for him. His parents took away his freedom, didn't listen to him and generally treated him like a child. At least that is the way he felt about it. So he asked a lot of people to pray for his parents to start understanding him. To him they weren't real Christians; all they apparently wanted was submission. After hearing a talk about prayer, he went to the Lord and asked Jesus to change him. Soon he saw how oversensitive he was to being dominated, how he didn't listen to his parents. The problem was that he wanted his own way around the house. He asked the Lord to help him die to this, and, as he puts it, "I watched my willfullness just melt away," as he started to love his parents. Within two weeks they granted him more freedom than he had fought for in the first place, and they even started to become friends.

What we found out about these situations was that we

needed "new eyes and new ears." We needed Jesus' help in prayer to see people the way He sees them. If somebody irritates us, we tend to give him a malicious motivation — we judge him. Jesus sees him as weak and wounded and in need of love. If we look at all people, even our enemies, as needing to be loved, then we just can't be defensive with them: they need *our* love. This is especially true of the people who intellectually, sexually or socially threaten us. If you think someone is cranky and always cutting people down, ask Jesus to help you see how insecure and fearful he might be. We can reach out to the child in someone because most of the time we don't feel threatened by a crying child — we want to help.

This demands absolute honesty in prayer. Of course, God knows us better than we know ourselves, so being honest is not to inform Him. What I mean is to be honest about your feelings. Don't try to act Christian or pious in your prayer. If you are angry, tell God. If you are depressed or despairing, share it with Jesus, who "can help those who are tempted, because he himself was tempted and suffered" (Hebrews 2:18 — TEV). The idea here is to tell Him what is bothering you and then to ask His Spirit to come and change your heart.

The way I have done this is just to tell Jesus something like: "Lord, he really gets me angry. I don't like him. I don't want to talk to him. I feel like punching him in the nose. And, I don't want to forgive him. So there (pout awhile). I really don't care if You loved him and died for that creep. I'm not going to forgive him." What happens is that after venting my frustration for a while, I start to realize how horribly I'm acting. I usually feel Jesus saying, "That's pretty mean all right, but I still love you." The result is that, instead of feeling guilty and brooding for days, I know I've been wrong but that I've been forgiven. At this point, I can start to take the log out of my own eye. This works powerfully, especially if you've planned to "tell someone off."

This whole attitude of praying for yourself is very positive. You're asking God to heal you so that you can love as He loves. This is exactly what God wants to do — make us loving people, Saints. Pray for your everyday situations and ask Jesus to give you the power of love. Ask Him to use you during the day to talk about His love. But know that He'll answer your prayers, sometimes in ways you don't expect. If you pray for patience, the Lord is likely to lead you into a situation which will test your patience to the limit. If you pray to be broken of your selfishness, you'll find yourself being contradicted and generally having to accept what other people want. At this point some people think God is trying to give them a hard time, when what He's really doing is answering their prayers to be a better lover. I am still amazed at the time I asked Jesus to help me love the people I felt were unlovable. The following week three people I couldn't stand asked to talk to me and have lunch, and inside of a month two more people moved into our house. I learned quickly what loving entails. This is not very glamorous, but it's very effective.

INTERCESSION

A great deal of our prayer time will be spent in praying for others. I like to think of this as a way of expressing my love for them. If someone asks for prayers, I'll think of him as I pray and ask God to help me see the good in him and to love him. Then I'll ask for the specific thing that he asked for. It helps as an exercise of faith to say, "Get Tom a job within a week, Lord." This just happened a few days ago, and Tom got a job on the seventh day. The more specific you get in praying for yourself and others, the easier it is to thank God for helping you. My father constantly amazes me with his faith in asking for parking places. I used to think this was silly, until one time I was moving and we had to take a rented trailer downtown. Neither of us could back it up, so we needed two car spaces on the end of the block. Four times in a row we got the end parking spot on a Saturday afternoon. I still don't know how or why that works.

If we don't know who or what to pray for, simply praise God or pray in tongues, for "the Spirit himself makes intercession for us with groanings which cannot be expressed in speech. He who searches hearts knows what the Spirit means, for the Spirit intercedes for the saints as God himself wills" (Romans 8:26, 27).

One of the biggest reasons why we don't pray for others is simply that we forget. I do this so often that now I try to keep a prayer list. What convinced me to do this was a man in a seminar I was teaching who asked us to pray for five sick friends of his. If I remember correctly their diseases were very serious — multiple sclerosis, brain tumor and things of that sort. A year later he came in and read off his list the story of how four of these people had been completely healed — either the symptoms disappeared or operations were successful. Then we could truly thank God. Both in praying for ourselves and praying for others, it takes time for us to truly trust God. As we experience our prayers being answered, then faith is based more on the fact of the Father's care for His children.

I want to add here some general observations about growing in our prayer life. The first thing is perseverance. There are going to be ups and downs in our relationship with Jesus, and it will take a long time for us to learn how to be faithful to Him. We will most probably fall, forget to pray, try to avoid Him in our guilt. This happens to everyone. What is important is that we persevere. We won't always feel like praying. Sometimes the best we can do is just sit there before God asking Him to help our unbelief. At times we'll feel it's all very silly, that we're just talking to the wall. We might think this to be useless, but as G. K. Chesterton once said, "Anything worth doing is worth doing poorly." It is better to pray poorly than not to pray at all. It is always better to love poorly than not to love at all. In prayer, this phase will pass, if we are faithful to spending time with Jesus. The big thing is not to stop trying to pray. If you forget to pray one day, turn to God now before guilt can overcome you. If you forget for two days, it's harder to return; after a week, even harder. Even if you stop praying for a month or a year, return to God. He always forgives, always lets you begin anew.

One of the best ways of persevering in prayer is to ask others to help you to pray. Most of all, the progress of our prayer life is something to share regularly with our confessor or spiritual director. We can also share our joys and problems in prayer with our friends. Doing this seems a bit uncomfortable at first, but after a while it's like asking a close friend how things are going with his fiancee. Sharing our prayer life helps us to have more faith and also gives us a healthy perspective on our own problems.

Most of what I've been saying has to do with daily time alone with Jesus. Because of this emphasis I've left out other valuable ideas on prayer that will appear in a later chapter. I want briefly to skim over some of these areas for the sake of balance and to encourage further study.

The first idea is praying throughout the day in some kind of ejaculatory or spontaneous prayer. Spending a structured time with God does not devalue spontaneous prayer. It's a question of both/and, not of either/or. What we have found is that, as the quality of our regular personal prayer deepens, we naturally talk to Jesus more frequently throughout the day. And the more we talk to Him throughout the day, the deeper our regular period of prayer becomes. This is the common sense dynamic of a friendship. The closer you get, the easier it is to dialogue or "rap." You become "tuned-in" to each other so that even if you chat for a few minutes, it's a real encounter. So then, many of the blank periods of our day can be encounters with Jesus. Waiting in lines, doctor's offices, boring manual work can all be moments shared with Jesus. To find out more about this, read *On Practicing the Presence of God* by Brother Lawrence.

Scripture also takes on a greater and greater meaning in our prayer. We've experienced that the more we seek to know Jesus, the more we are led to pray, meditate and study the Scriptures. This might be done in a structured period each day or incorporated into our prayer time. Scripture is the basic way that God speaks to us. It is understood only in the power of the Spirit who "leads us into all the truth." We've found that Scripture comes alive in prayer when we beg the Spirit to teach us how this applies to our lives. Inspirational books like *That Man Is You* by Louis Evely or *Repentance — the Joy-filled Life* by M. Basilea Schlink have helped me a lot to prayerfully read the Scriptures.

BARRIERS TO PRAYER

Focusing on giving God an hour a day also creates an impression that our prayer life is somehow cut off from our everyday life. Actually, personal prayer is only one aspect of giving our whole life to God. Work, friendship, group prayer, Eucharist and study are all integrated with our personal prayer to build a full friendship with God. To clarify this further, I want to list some common obstacles to prayer as we've experienced it in our community.

1. Life Style — Having an excessively chaotic and disorganized life robs us of the peace that the Lord wants to give us. This includes the great American tradition of business or activity for activity's sake. Competitiveness and perfectionism makes us feel that we're only worthwhile if we're doing something. Living this way, we will probably never find the time to pray; or if we do, we'll rarely be able to relax enough to seriously encounter God. This means that we have to reevaluate what we do with our time. Some activities, books or even friends will have to go, so that our life will be conducive to union with God.

2. Bad Relationships — Usually we found that having an unforgiving heart or holding a grudge will effectively destroy our relationship with Jesus after a while. What happens is that we value our hurt and bitterness more than the Lord who asks us to forgive and pray for our enemies. This also applies to selfish relationships of all sorts — treating a friend or a spouse as a Savior, consistent dishonesty or isolation, sexual selfishness. Unless our heart is right with our neighbor, our heart won't be right with God.

3. Introspection — An excessive preoccupation with our own guilt and problems leaves us no time to turn to God. Scrupulosity and constant worry are so self-centered that we can rarely focus on Jesus and "seek first the Kingdom of God."

4. Getting into a Rut — Basically this is placing too much emphasis on the externals of prayer. Confusing the means and the end, we lose sight of the real purpose of encountering and loving God. This will naturally happen from time to time, but by being aware of it we can avoid a lot of problems. What it amounts to is a communication breakdown with Jesus. Now if a

91

married couple experienced this, they, hopefully, go to someone to help them explore ways of re-establishing communication. They will use any means available to do this. It's the same with prayer — we need to be free and experimental as regards communication techniques. If it helps, use it; if it doesn't, try something else. What's important is that we come into union with God.

5. **Seeking Spiritual Experiences** — If we want to get high on Jesus more than we want Jesus, we'll find neither. Love creates joy and peace when we focus on the beloved, not on the effect of that love. To seek spiritual experiences is like maintaining a friendship with someone because he or she gives beautiful gifts. There is nothing wrong with the gifts, but everything wrong with the motive.

6. **Impatience** — Expecting too much too soon leads to rapid discouragement. This is trying to force yourself to be holy when only God can do it. Usually impatience expresses itself in an excessive use of devotional techniques, fasts, and mortification, in scrupulosity and a lack of humor. It is taking yourself too seriously and not taking seriously enough the Lord's gift of love.

Most of these obstacles to a loving union have to do with problems of behavior in our everyday life. Confession and inner healing are needed most so that we can be free to be friends with Jesus.

AN EVER DEEPENING RELATIONSHIP

This connection between our life and prayer is completed when we think of what the result or fruit of prayer is. St. Augustine said, "He who prays well lives well." Loving prayer leads to a loving life. This is the absolute criterion of all our Christian actions. There's no way around it. This also means that loving Jesus in prayer is the school where we learn how to love our neighbor.

As we grow in our experience of the love of Jesus in prayer, it is natural that we gradually relate to different aspects of His personality. I began my relationship with Jesus experiencing Him as my friend and brother. Slowly I came to appreciate what Savior meant, and then, Jesus as Lord. Eventually, as I experienced the power and transcendence of God through the Charismatic Renewal, I felt the awe and unworthiness of standing before the "Holy One of Israel" — the God who is God. I met God as the Almighty and as the Father who cares for me as a son. Most of all, right now I relate to the intimate and passionate love of the Bridegroom who says to his beloved, "Come, the wedding feast is prepared."

This is what happens in all deep relationships. The person becomes a mystery — infinitely discoverable. As this happens with God, our prayer becomes less what Louis Evely calls "a speech we make to God" and more a discovery of who God is. Silence and stillness grow as God takes more of the initiative and we learn to accept Him as He is — a lover.

Married partners go through this discovery when they reach the point of saying, "After ten years I really don't know you." We box each other in, only to be surprised at finding a new person to love. So we grow close to Jesus, continually surprised at the friend who is our lover and the lover who is our King, Savior and God. And slowly our life becomes characterized by a constant theme of joy which sings to the world simply and confidently: "My lover belongs to me and I to him" (Song of Songs 2:16).

As a brief summary, here's a little scheme to remember:
1. **Perseverance** — in scheduled daily prayer time.
2. **Place** — to be alone and free from distractions.
3. **Posture** — to express inner attitude.
4. **Practicalities** — are always important.
5. **Praise** — and thank God spontaneously in the Spirit.
6. **Presence** — of God encountered in love by focusing on Jesus.
7. **Petition** — for yourself in honesty and others in love.
8. **Power** — of the Holy Spirit is what makes prayer possible.

BIBLIOGRAPHY
RECOMMENDED READING:
Hunter, Francis Gardiner, *Hotline to Heaven*, Warner Press, Anderson, Indiana, 1970, 96pp.
  A how-to book on prayer, filled with examples.

Lawrence, Brother, *The Practice of the Presence of God,* Spire Books, Old Tappen, New Jersey, 1958, 63pp.
The classic of simple love and friendship with God as lived by a 17th century monk.

Rinker, Rosalind, *Prayer: Conversing with God,* Zondervan, Grand Rapids, Michigan, 1959, 117pp.
Although primarily for small group prayer, this book has so much practical and personal wisdom about having a conversation with Jesus that it deserves to be read.

SUPPLEMENTARY READING:
Evely, Louis, *Teach Us How to Pray,* Paulist-Newman, Paramus, New Jersey, 1973, 106pp.
A sound, strong book which helps us listen to God.

Leheux, Martin, O.F.M., *The Art of Prayer,* Franciscan Press, Chicago, 1959, 306pp.
A complete and practical guide to union with God, which covers conversational prayer, meditation, effective prayer and contemplation.

by Tony Cushing

Conversational Prayer ⑥

Where two or three are gathered in my name, there am I in their midst.

(Matt. 18:20)

The Church, the people of God, are the people who've experienced the good news that God loves them more than they could ever hope for. To accept this amazing love of God in the person of Jesus is to be transported from our loneliness, isolation and fear to the peace and joy of being worthwhile and loved. This is the Church (*ekklesia*): "the people called out" of isolation to share a life of love and service. These are the people who have been liberated from fear, phoniness, insecurity, in order that the love of God can overflow to others:

that all may be one
as you, Father, are in me, and I in you;
. . .
I living in them, you living in me—
that their unity may be complete.
So shall the world know that you sent me,
and that you loved them as you loved me.

(John 17:21 & 23)

It is overwhelming that Jesus prays for us to be one-in-love as He and the Father are one-in-love. You even get the impression that Jesus expects His followers to experience more than a little of this loving oneness. Over the years, one also gets the impression that Christians' failure to love in this way has been almost as fantastic and as overwhelming as the promise of Jesus' prayer. It is obvious that a great many Catholics do not experience being completely one when they come together in

95

the Eucharist (Communion!). If anything, there have been widespread rumors that the Mass and group prayer "don't mean anything any more." People say they "don't get anything out of it." I think what people mean by this is that they don't experience anything significant at liturgical gatherings. It doesn't touch them or meet their personal needs. It isn't relevant to their lives. I understand this feeling because I once felt that way. But I and thousands of others have discovered a solution to this "meaninglessness" of church life and worship. Not surprisingly, this answer is simply Jesus.

When I say Jesus is the answer, I don't mean to be cute or to impute sinfulness to those who feel this lack of relevance. I simply imply a return to the basics of what it means to be a Christian community. To me, that means sharing Jesus, in love and prayer.

Community — the common union — means that our basic relationship is to share the loving oneness we have with Jesus. "I am the vine, you are the branches . . . apart from me you can do nothing" (John 15:5). This is something that must be *lived*. It has to do with how we act toward each other, what we talk about, what we share together. A seminarian expressed it perfectly on a retreat we were giving a few years ago: "I can't share all my cultural, intellectual or social interests with all of you. That would be impossible. What I can share with all of you is my relationship with Jesus; this is what we all experience."

PRAYER IN SMALL GROUPS

What I want to do is to talk about one part of the general solution — small group prayer. It might be a very small part of what it means to share Jesus, but it's one that has significantly made me better able to experience and share the love of God.

The relationship we share with Jesus has the same dynamics as any human relationship of friendship and love. It takes time, effort, discipline, and, most of all, love. Fundamental to any friendship is the time you spend alone with someone (personal prayer). There are also times you celebrate together with others in parties or festivals (the Mass as the Wedding Banquet). Other times you get together with a few close friends to share on a deeper, more intimate level (small group prayer or Eucharist). Each kind of grouping has its own dynamics. For example, the things you talk about and do at a large party are much different from what you say and do with a group of intimate friends. So, as I talk about small group prayer, keep in mind that what I describe might not apply to other kinds of prayer gatherings. This is not to say that I don't approve of or enjoy other forms of prayer (I do). It just means that for now I want to limit myself to that style of prayer for small groups called conversational or shared prayer.

The basic value of small group prayer is that we can encounter Jesus in an intimate and related way that meets our personal needs. This is something you can't do easily at Mass or a large prayer meeting. First of all, there simply isn't time for everyone to pray for his needs. Secondly, most people wouldn't want to risk doing that in so large and anonymous a group.

The basic idea underlying this kind of prayer is that Jesus is *really present* to us "whenever two or three" are gathered, and that *we can talk to Him.* It's very simple. It's having a conversation with Jesus and a group of friends.

As to how you go about doing this, I would refer you to an expert on prayer by the name of Rosalind Rinker. We have been using her method of conversational prayer for the last three and a half years and the results have been beautiful. Most of what I have to say about this kind of prayer will be based on her books: *Prayer: Conversing with God* and *Communicating Love Through Prayer,* which I highly recommend. I'll also be sharing some of our community experience with this kind of prayer. But at this point I want to go into what it means to encounter Jesus in prayer and to experience the presence of God.

PRESENCE

Religious experience is first of all a human experience. And there are all kinds of ways that we experience the presence of another person. There's the face to face encounter where we rely on sight, touch and hearing. You experience a different kind of presence when you are talking to someone on the telephone or reading a letter. There are certain kinds of an unexplainable sense of presence when someone stares at your back and your hair prickles, or when you come into a supposed empty house and you "know" there's somebody on the third floor. You can experience a person you don't directly encounter. This is like the flash of presence and warmth you might feel when you suddenly think of an old friend whom you miss. The point here is that when I talk about experiencing the presence of God, I'm not necessarily referring to a vision or something like that. The experience, though, is very real.

What I mean by presence is the experiencing and awareness of another person. This is very different from a minimal physical encounter. You can be on a crowded street and physically encounter many people who are not present to you. You're not aware of them as persons. All of us have known self-centered people who just "aren't there" when you talk to them. They aren't aware of you as a person. Their attention is on themselves, so they're really not present to you. We know this all the more when we experience the joy of real presence and dialogue with another person. It's exciting, dynamic and most of all, you forget about yourself. If you haven't experienced this, it's almost impossible to describe. Think of all the endless love poetry trying to describe a fairly common experience. Yet unless a person has been in love, the poetry cannot create the experience for him — it's literally not understandable. Describing religious or loving experience is much like what Count Basie said about rhythm, "If you've got it, no definition is necessary; if you don't have it, no definition will help." The basics we learn from our everyday life: to experience the presence of God is first of all *to focus your attention on a person who loves you.*

Now I'm not using the words "presence of God" to suggest something with a mystical connotation. I suspect that most of those who read this will have experienced the loving presence of Jesus in one way or another. This experiencing is part and parcel of the Catholic tradition which prays, "Come, Holy Spirit, fill us with the fire of your divine love," and "Happy are those who are called to this supper." Yet for a lot of us this encounter with Jesus might be only a distant memory or a rare occurrence. The question is: how do we make the experience of God's transforming love a staple reality of our life? More particularly, how do we share this experience in praying together? This was precisely the dilemma that Rosalind Rinker found herself in when she "discovered" conversational prayer.

CONVERSATIONAL PRAYER

Rosalind Rinker was a missionary in China. She was trying to pray, yet the prayer meetings she went to "didn't mean anything" to her. She found them boring because there were always the same "experts" praying those long, stilted prayers. She also felt threatened because she wanted to pray but feared she would make a fool of herself. She didn't know how to pray those beautiful stylized prayers. Out of all of this "lack of meaning" she realized the need for a simple conversational prayer form in which everyone participated. After years of experimenting with this small group prayer, she found that structuring it into four steps helped people to be more comfortable praying. They are: (1) imagining Jesus present, (2) thanking Jesus, (3) asking Jesus for help and forgiveness, and (4) asking Jesus to help my brother. I want to describe how these four steps to small group prayer work.

Step 1: Imagining Jesus present. This is one of the oldest meditation techniques (e.g., rosary, stations of the cross). It's purpose is to help us focus our attention on Jesus. Most of us feel that imaginative distractions are a big barrier to prayer. What you do here is simply use your imagination to help you focus on Jesus.

First of all, relax. After all, you're going to have a conversation with your friend, Jesus. He knows everything about you, so you don't have to be formal. Sit together in a comfortable place; smoke, drink coffee if you want to. Generally make yourself at home.

Realize that you have come together to experience Jesus' promise that whenever two or three of you are together, He will be there. Welcome Him. Spend some time in silence to help you become aware of His presence. Imagine what Jesus would be doing if He were physically present in the room. What would He look like? The first time I did this, I got this vivid picture of

Jesus sitting in the corner smiling this big Cheshire-cat grin. And then He laughed and laughed this great-big, Oh-What-a-Joy-Life-Is laugh. It just made you want to join in and be healed by His laughter. A friend of mine just imagined seeing Jesus's feet, cut and dirty from the road, and somehow he just wanted to help Jesus and to follow Him. Others imagine Him on the cross, or on the road talking to the apostles, or working as a carpenter. Some people imagine Jesus as a sense of peace or warmth or as sunshine on a spring day. It doesn't really matter what the content of your meditation picture is; the idea is to focus your attention on the physical presence of Jesus.

Each person will probably have a different picture of Jesus which springs from his own unique approach to God. When each one shares his own imagining of Jesus, it enriches everybody else's experience of Jesus' presence. It sometimes creates a lot of laughter. The big point is for everyone in the group to *share out loud* how they imagine Jesus.

Step 2: Thanking Jesus. When you finish the first step of entering into at least the imaginative presence of Jesus, then you talk to Him, again out loud. Remember this a *conversation,* so all the regular sensitivities of conversation apply. First of all, you talk loud enough for everyone to hear. Secondly, you don't monopolize the conversation, but you give everyone a chance to talk. Most importantly, it is a conversation with Jesus, directed *to* Jesus. This means that you use His name. If you want to thank Him for the springtime weather, say, "Thank you, Jesus, for springtime weather." The conversation is always directed to Jesus. If you want to discuss something, stop praying and discuss it. Don't change a prayer group into a discussion group. In directing the conversation to Jesus, we also find it helpful when *everyone responds* to a person's prayer. If someone prays, "Thank you, Jesus, for Irene's friendship," everyone else responds, "Yes, thank you, Jesus, for Irene." This is not meant to be a mechanical chorus, but rather a way of recognizing and joining in with another person's prayer of thanks.

You can thank Jesus for anything and everything. Thank Him for your family, your health, good meals, friends. Thank Jesus for the little things that happen throughout the day — at work, school, around the house. "Every worthwhile gift, every genuine benefit comes from above" (James 1:17), so thank Jesus for anything that He's given you. I knew a guy who used to thank Jesus for door knobs. He had a very large collection of door knobs which he really liked, so he wanted to thank Jesus for those door knobs. It also helps the group to pray if you thank Jesus for each other. Prayer itself is a gift and so are the people you pray with, so thank Jesus for them. "Thank you, Jesus, for Jimmy's laugh," or "Thank you, Jesus, for how pretty Carol looks today." Praying in this way allows us to communicate our love to each person in the group.

Simplicity is also a major aid toward meaningful prayer. We found that a lot of people are afraid to pray aloud because of a fear that they would appear foolish or say the wrong thing. Many of us were intimidated by people who were extravagant pray-ers. We found out that the *more simple and natural* the prayer is, the more meaningful it is. For example, in the "Thank you" stage, it is better to thank Jesus for one thing at a time. If you have ten things to thank Him for, thank Him ten different times while giving others a chance to join in the "conversation." And in thanking Jesus, it's best not to editorialize or try to explain why something means so much to you. Use simple declarative sentences like, "Thank you, Jesus, for Chris' gift." Keep it simple.

Thanking Jesus for the good things He gives us helps to build up our trust in God. As we remember and believe how Jesus has worked in our life, we can expect in faith that He really will hear our prayer. Praying, out loud, together, helps to increase the faith of the whole group. As I hear what Jesus has done for you, I can also expect Him to work in my life in a similar way. At times I won't be trusting God very much, but when I go and pray with others their faith helps me to have faith. Praying with others, I can see and hear in them how trusting in God works for the best.

Step 3: Asking Jesus for help and forgiveness. After welcoming Jesus and thanking Him for a while, it is only natural to want to talk to Him about your personal needs. For most people this is the most difficult part of conversational prayer.

Yet we have found through experience that this is the *most important part* of praying together. It consists of asking for forgiveness, healing, help for our weaknesses, etc. It is ultimately personal and, in a way, humbling. You take the risk of exposing your own weakness and sinfulness. It is asking other people to accept you as you are and to pray that you might be changed. This means that you have to *trust* that the other people really do love and accept you.

Most people are afraid of doing this. We all want to appear to be good and perfect Christians. We like the security of our virtue and our social masks. As a result, many people try to dodge this step in prayer. The easiest way to avoid revealing yourself is to pray for others. So people say, "Well, wouldn't it be selfish to pray for myself? I mean, there are more important things than my problems." This might be true, but it doesn't mean that your Father, who loves you and "has numbered the hairs on your head" and "knows that you need all these things," doesn't care about your small problems. "If anyone among you is suffering hardship, he must pray ... Hence, declare your sins to one another, and pray for one another, that you may find healing" (James 5:13, 16). We Christians are to love one another as Jesus did — revealing ourselves, sharing our weakness as well as our goodness.

Another way of avoiding self-revelation is the editorial "we." Some people do this by praying, "Jesus, forgive *us* our pride in achievement," instead of, "Jesus, forgive *me* my pride in achievement." This is a real cop-out because you think you've sneaked in a prayer for yourself while avoiding the risk of disclosing your weakness. Well, in the first place it seems kind of judgmental to assume that the others in the group are prideful. I mean, how do you know what's in their heart? And Jesus says, "How can you say to your brother, 'Let me take that speck out of your eye,' while all the time the plank remains in your own? You hyprocrite! Remove the plank from your own eye first; then you will see clearly to take the speck from your brother's eye" (Matt. 7:4-5). So, first ask Jesus to forgive you and help you in *your* weakness before you ask Him to help others' weaknesses. Each of us must always say, "Help *me,* have mercy on *me,* a sinner" before we can pray, "Help *us* sinners."

Again, the key words here are *honesty* and *simplicity*. Don't try to explain why you did something wrong; just ask for forgiveness. If you were selfish and inconsiderate to your friend, don't say, "Lord, I was so misunderstood today, blah, blah, blah." Tell it like it is and confess your wrongdoing. If you hated someone, say so and don't try to ignore the plank in your own eye. If you were lusting for someone, say just that and ask for forgiveness. This isn't scandalous or upsetting to people. Scandal is when you expose someone else's wrongdoing without his permission. Here you're only talking about your own sinfulness, your own problems. And far from upsetting people, this honesty helps us in the faith. Whenever someone is humble enough to confess something in a group prayer, I too am humbled and at the same time built up in my faith. When we all do this, we can relax in the fact of our common sinfulness. We are all weak and therefore we can all rejoice in the forgiveness of Jesus.

Also, letting people know me in this way means that I can relax and be myself with them. I don't have to wear a mask. Also, I can air out the problems, doubts and resentments that otherwise might gnaw away at my peace. As John Powell wrote in *Why Am I Afraid to Love?:* "When you repress or suppress those things which you don't want to live with, you don't really solve the problem because you don't bury the problem dead — *you bury it alive."* (It remains alive and active inside of you.)

This is not mere group therapy. It is asking God and others for forgiveness, which just happens to work out as great group therapy. It is not discussion; it is prayer. So when someone asks Jesus for help and forgiveness, everyone in the group should pray for that person. If he offended you, express your love and forgiveness. "Yes, Lord, Jimmy really was selfish today, but I forgive him, Jesus, and I ask you to help him experience your forgiveness right now."

Recognizing the problem, don't try to make light of it. If someone has done something wrong, accept it as wrong, and love and forgive the person. This is, after all, the way that God loves us. After a while, as we experience that we are loved even when we do things wrong, we'll even believe that we're O.K. and loved for who we really are. That is one of the most liberating things that can ever happen.

Step 4: Asking Jesus to help my brother. As we are united in the presence of Jesus as weak, sinful people who need His help, then we can pray with faith for others. "If two of you join your voices on earth to pray for anything whatever, it shall be granted you" (Matt. 18:19).

> Ask, and you will receive. Seek, and you will find. Knock, and it will be opened to you . . . . Would one of you hand his son a stone when he asks for a loaf, or a poisonous snake when he asks for a fish? If you, with all your sins, know how to give your children what is good, how much more will your heavenly Father give good things to anyone who asks him!
>
> (Matt. 7:7, 9-11)

Praying for others is a basic way to express our love and concern for people. It is also a manifestation of our faith in the care and love of our Father. This too is all part of the conversation we have with Jesus, and it still maintains the attitudes of simplicity, honesty and naturalness that I talked about earlier.

It also helps to be very specific in what you pray for. This enables us to see how God is active in a particular situation. If we pray for world peace, we can trust that God is doing something; but it is doubtful that we can see a definite answer to our prayers. Praying for concrete needs gives us the opportunity to know God is working and also gives us more reason to thank Him when our prayers are answered.

This was really evident in a class I was running where we were praying in small groups together. One of the men needed a part-time job. He was married, going to school, and the only time he could work was in the early morning hours. We prayed that he'd get a job soon, and for some reason I felt inspired to ask Jesus to do it within a week. When we got together the next week, he said he hadn't been able to find a job until the day before, when a local restaurant owner had called him and said he needed someone to work the early morning hours part-time. It was fantastic. The man's financial situation cleared up a bit, and we all wanted to thank God for what He had done.

Sometimes, you might want to pray for a person outside the group. You might need to explain what the situation is, so just take time to do this so that the whole group knows what to pray for. If it is a serious thing, we should try to keep it anonymous at all costs. It is not necessary for prayer to know that "the man who beats his wife" is really your brother-in-law. To "explain" this is not love; it is simply being scandalous.

Occasionally also, you might want to pray for someone in the group. I find it very beautiful when people pray for my needs. I really feel loved. It shows that people care about what happens to me and that they actually remember something that might be bothering me. Such a prayer can also be very humbling and revealing, because it shows how other people see your problems. One time a young girl prayed, "Jesus, help Tony not to be so abstract when he talks." It was true and I had to accept it. It can also be enlightening when you pray for yourself and others obviously agree with what's wrong. This happens with people who really know you, as when I prayed to overcome my "insensitivity to domestic values," and my roommate prayed, "Oh yes, Lord, help Tony not to be so sloppy." I just couldn't hide behind my nice words.

Obviously, this can be done in a wrong way that smacks of self-righteousness. The key here is love. St. Paul says that if we "profess the truth in love . . . the whole body grows" (Eph. 4:15, 16). Well, it's the same when you pray for others. You have the right to speak the truth only when it's in love. A prayer that rejoices over another's weakness is clearly not prayer. By speaking the truth (about ourselves and others) in love, our prayer will be compassionate and sensitive to others' needs. It will also be powerful, since when we love, the Holy Spirit of Love works through us.

One of the things I like about asking poeple to pray for my needs in a small group is that I can really expect them to pray in faith. The reason for this is that over the course of three years we have seen so many prayers answered that we have grown in trusting God through the experience of His goodness. This trust, like any other relationship, takes time to develop. I can remember when our prayer group had just got started, and a woman prayed for a baby to be healed. The child had spinal meningitis and hadn't spoken or stood up throughout the three years of his life. The child was in the hospital, and the mother was a nervous wreck. So the woman prayed that "something definite happen tommorow." The next morning the child stood up in the crib and started talking. Coincidentally, the doctors could find no further evidence of the spinal meningitis.

We saw many more small miracles — from being able to overcome shyness to having cracked engine blocks not overheat on a 500-mile trip. We have, through this experience of answered prayer, learned a positive aspect of the prayer of petition. This is the prayer that Jesus be with us in things that really aren't problems at all. So we ask Him to help us have really good friends, to have a joyful time at a party or to increase a married couple's love. This is basically having faith in the Lord's promise that He came that we "might have life, and have it to the full" (John 10:10).

DYNAMICS

We have also learned a lot about the dynamics of small group prayer. We found that the big things are: to relax, talk to Jesus simply as a friend, pray for yourself, and pray in faith.

The more relaxed and real the prayer becomes, the better it is. We need to be ourselves in prayer. This was illustrated beautifully by a group of seminarians in Washington. After being instructed in how to pray this way, they went off determined to have a meaningful, relaxed prayer. The result was forty minutes of stilted, uncomfortable, forced prayer. After it was over and they had relaxed from the "ordeal," someone remembered something he wanted to pray for. They prayed for another forty minutes and it was a beautiful, open and natural prayer. The key was their relaxed attitude which helped them to experience and talk to Jesus as a friend.

There a number of things that help us to be relaxed and natural when we pray together. The first is song. Singing one or

106

two hymns of praise at the beginning of prayer helps us to make a conscious break from discussion into prayer. The more spontaneous the song becomes, the more relaxing it is. Just the very fact of using our voices helps us to be more natural about talking to Jesus.

We also find that it helps to follow the four-step format of prayer — at least until we're comfortable enough to pray completely spontaneously. These steps almost seem to be the natural progression toward a deeper experience of prayer. For example, if we start praying for others before we pray for ourselves, we would usually skip that difficult but fruitful prayer for personal needs. There is a certain flow to a prayer group, and we need to be sensitive to the way the Holy Spirit leads us in prayer. Sometimes, there might be a great deal of silence which is peaceful and comforting. Other times the silence might be simply the tension caused by the fear of opening up. We don't have to be afraid of the peaceful silence. Prayer is *listening* to God as well as talking to Him. But in the times of "tense" silence, we need to be honest with each other. Maybe someone will just pray, "Jesus, I'm really uncomfortable — help me to pray." This usually breaks the ice and everyone can relax.

As we became more real in our prayer together, we found that we experience many different emotional aspects to prayer. Sometimes a person might truly experience his sinfulness for the first time and just cry and cry all through the prayer time. We found it helps if we responded naturally and accepted this person's feelings and prayed for him right then. You might embrace the person or hold his hand and thank Jesus for his tears and his honesty. Responding in this way enables a person to experience the forgiveness of Jesus. Most of the time this kind of tears leads to very clean smiles of relief.

I've also prayed with groups where everyone might start crying out of sheer joy — and that's fantastic. There's also a lot of laughter and downright good humor. Most of this is because prayer helps us not to take ourselves too seriously. I remember one time when we had been holding hands and praying for about an hour; someone brought the house down by praying, "Thank you, Jesus, for sweaty palms." Prayer can be fun.

Jesus said that He was like a bridegroom to us and that we were His friends. We should keep in mind that on our side of our relationship with Him we will have the joys, sorrows, problems of communication, and emotions that all friendships have.

BUILDING TRUST

Conversational prayer really starts to bear fruit after a group has been doing it regularly, like once a week for a few months. The reason for this is that most people at first feel awkward praying out loud, and it takes a while to get comfortable enough to pray for important things. Time builds trust, and as we experience the love of a group and witness answered prayers, we can have more and more faith in God and each other. Sometimes it's good to pray with a group of friends who have already reached a level of trust for each other. We need this if we are to expose our deepest fears and problems to God and to each other in prayer. We also recommend that everything that goes on in a prayer group remain anonymous and confidential, unless someone gives permission to share a particular incident. It's just loving to keep secret something that a friend has entrusted to you in the privacy of prayer.

As a group prays together over a period of time, we find that it is very easy to lose the sense of simple honesty with each other. One cause of this is that some prayer meetings are simply a bore. People might be tired or distracted and consequently never really seek Jesus' presence. This happens from time to time and is to be expected. There are other times when we find that conversational prayer gets dry, wearisome, and meaningless. We found that this usually happens when we stop praying for our personal needs. It just seems that whenever we leave out the *help me, Jesus,* aspect, the prayer goes flat. Thank God that someone usually complains about feeling phony, and that leads all of us to confess and to once more be real with Jesus and each other.

Sometimes we feel that we can't open up in prayer simply because there is no depth of trust in the group. This might result from a lack of time together or because new people are present. For example, if four people pray together every week for a few months, they have established some depth of trust in each other. If a stranger were to come every week for a month, our group would probably find the prayer getting impersonal. The sharing in any group is only as deep as the newest or least-advanced member. Groups naturally settle at the lowest common denominator of communication. You can see this happen whenever you are reminiscing with a group of old friends and a new person comes in — the whole conversation changes. If this continues, as in our example group, the people would experience what sociologists describe as the "tired phase." As new people enter the group, the group has to relate to them. If this happens week after week, the group has no chance to grow together; it is always reaching out. This is a practical reason for some prayer groups to be "closed," or limited to certain people, so that its members can grow together. As long as you keep these problems of growth in mind, you can organize your small prayer group any way you like.

The more we mature in trust and openness, the more deeply the Lord can heal us in our minds and hearts. We find that this works best when prayer becomes a regular part of our friendships, marriages, and work relationships. This is to say that prayer is usually a richer experience with those with whom you already have a trusting, open relationship. This kind of prayer is also much riskier and more difficult. When you pray together one-to-one with someone who knows you, you just can't be phony. You have to be yourself, forgiving and humble with the very person who may have hurt you and judged you the most. Many married couples find it difficult to pray together. This is also true of close friends or people who are dating or engaged. This prayer is risky and threatening because it touches the deepest parts of our personality. Just by praying together in this way, though, you are opening the door so Jesus can heal your deepest fears and anxieties. As the relationship becomes more and more based on the love of God, you are challenged to give up possessiveness, resentment, judgments, etc., so that the Lord can heal you. This is the most powerful kind of prayer that we have experienced.

SHARING LIFE

Generally, we found that our prayer together is as profound as the degree to which we share our lives together. Many times when we teach in other communities, we find that people who have been attending prayer meetings for a long time still feel isolated and unloved. Part of the reason for this is that they never developed any friendships with the people they prayed with nor did they pray with their friends. Their prayer life never touched the deepest fears and sinfulness (isolation) of their lives. To experience community prayer to the fullest, you not only have to pray together but you need to share your everyday life together. We have a motto: "to really pray together you have to play together." You can go to prayer meetings regularly, but if no one really knows who you are, chances are that the prayer will lose its power to transform you. Loving God with our whole hearts, souls, and minds means that we have to let Him into our whole hearts, souls and minds.

This is what conversational prayer can do. It allows Jesus, in the power of the Spirit, to transform the very personal and intimate recesses of our lives. We all need this. We also need the unbelievable Presence of the Eucharist, the joy of large prayer meetings and daily private prayer to build the friendship with Jesus. We need to relate to Jesus in all the possibilities of our everyday lives and relationships. In this way we will start to realize, right now, what it means to be "completely one" even as Jesus and the Father are one.

BIBLIOGRAPHY

RECOMMENDED READING:

Rinker, Rosalind, *Prayer: Conversing with God,* Zondervan, Grand Rapids, Michigan, 1959, 117pp.

The method and value of simple, relaxed, small-group prayer. Filled with personal witness.

Rinker, Rosalind, *Communicating Love through Prayer,* Zondervan, Grand Rapids, Michigan, 1966, 127pp.

More practical guidelines for making small-group prayer meaningful.

by Joseph Lange

The Gift of the Spirit   7

In the general theological perspective, we pointed out that the core of the Good News is that the Father sent the Son and together They sent the Holy Spirit so that each of us might know that he is totally known and totally loved. Each of the four canons of the Roman Liturgy prays that we might be filled with the Holy Spirit. In Canon IV it reads: "And that we might live no longer for ourselves but for him, he sent the Holy Spirit from you, Father, as his first gift to those who believe, to complete his work on earth and bring us the fullness of grace."

To many of us, these are references to a mysterious Being, even though we profess faith in the Holy Spirit in our various Creeds. As a boy I remember listening to sermons on "The Holy Spirit, the Unknown Person of the Trinity," sermons which left me as uninformed as I was before I heard them. I am not blaming the preachers. We just didn't know much about the Spirit in those days. In my own seminary days we never had a single hour of class devoted to the Holy Spirit! Several years after I was ordained, I was asked to give a retreat to a group of Sisters whose congregation was dedicated to the Holy Spirit. I thought it would be a good idea to give one talk on the Holy Spirit, so I looked up whatever I could find, only to discover that there was very little in the available Catholic literature on the subject. In research for an earlier book I happened to read Schillebeeckx's book *Christ, the Sacrament of the Encounter with God.* In it he wrote that through baptism we become part of the Body of Christ; through confirmation we become established in power. I liked that so I included it in my book, but I didn't understand it!

111

Some years later I was invited to hear a Pentecostal preacher and to be prayed with for the "baptism of the Spirit." At the time I knew very little about that. I knew a priest who had read the Ranaghans' book *Catholic Pentecostals* and said that he thought it was orthodox theologically. I also knew that Steve Clark and Ralph Martin had become involved in this Pentecostalism, and I had grown to respect both of them for their dedication to the Lord as well as for their learning and maturity. My impression of this "baptism of the Spirit" was that it enabled one to experience the gifts of the Spirit enjoyed by the early Church. The impression was vague, but it was clear enough to make me want to look into it someday. The day had arrived with this invitation, and at first I made excuses about not having time and that sort of thing. But persuasion prevailed and off I went to a Pentecostal meeting.

By this time in my life I had been ordained about ten years. I had earnestly sought to serve God, and I had been preaching about Jesus, and I had been calling people to a personal knowledge and love of Him. I wasn't praying as faithfully as I might, but I was praying. I had a lot of my own ideas about how to bring people to Christ, and I was energetic in pursuing these programs on a college campus and elsewhere. I also felt a little cheated by God. I had always wanted to believe that "the greater things than these" that Christ had promised us, we too should be able to expect. But, somehow, I never met anyone or any group for whom that promise was real. As I drove to that meeting I had a vague feeling that this "baptism of the Spirit" would give me the faith for this. I also remember experiencing some fear that this whole thing might be something demonic, so I prayed, "Lord, if this is of You, then I want whatever You want to give me. If this is not of You, protect me."

Skipping over the details, I was prayed for that night in a room full of about fifty rather extraordinary people. To me, what was extraordinary was that for the first time in my life I had encountered a whole group of people who not only believed that they could expect God to give them gifts of tongues and prophecy and miracles and healings, but who were experiencing these things in their lives. In the company of those faith-full people my own faith expanded, and I joined them in praising God in tongues.

Over the next few weeks I began to experience a strong desire to pray, a new and personally exciting relevance in my reading of Scripture and the prayers of the Mass, a gradually deepening peace, and a deep sense of faith. I began to feel that I was beginning to understand how the early Christians felt and how the Saints felt. I also began to sense a new power in my preaching, a power that was not there before, a power that was showing itself by the way in which my sermons were touching people. Another insight which came to me with a forceful clarity was that I had not really been following Jesus; rather, I had been doing my own thing and inviting Jesus to bless it. So I let go of my projects and began to look for His will for me.

All of this led me to a rather intensive study of Scripture and of Pentecostal literature and to workshops and meetings around the country, to be with others who were discovering the same things. It became clear that we were encountering the power of the Gospel in a new-yet-old-way — and we were excited. What follows are some of the things we have learned and are still learning.

I believe it is not premature to point out here that Pentecostalism is not the total answer to the revival of the Church. There is truth, God-given truth, in the power of the Spirit, and we owe a debt to Pentecostalism for awakening us to that truth. But the Spirit is also at work in many other areas of the Church and between the churches. We must not mistake the part for the whole, but neither must we neglect a fundamental part. As the Liturgical Renewal has done, the Charismatic Renewal is simply awakening the Church to what is fundamental to her heritage. It is not the whole of renewal; it is only part of the renewal.

I firmly believe that each person initiated into the Church through baptism and confirmation has been given the Spirit. The power of the Spirit is released through faith, expectant faith. The so-called "baptism in the Spirit" means "immersion" in the Spirit, the process of a lifetime. The Spirit had been at work in my life (and has been in yours) for many years prior to my being prayed with. I believe that what happened to me was that I encountered a body of believing Christians whose faith encouraged me to believe. These people taught me to expect more — and God answered our expectant faith. The purpose of each chapter of this book is to describe what God wants for us so that we might believe and choose Him and His gifts. Belief in all that He wants for us makes it possible for Him to give us all He wants for us.

That much being said, let's look at the Holy Spirit.

THE HOLY SPIRIT

The word in Hebrew which is translated as "Spirit" is *ruah*. McKenzie points out that *ruah* is really untranslatable by any single word. It's also variously translated as "wind," "breath," and "power," but it never means just one of those things; it means all of these at once. So the Spirit of God is the breath or wind or power of God, the source of life, the source of wisdom, the source of power. It was this Spirit which "anointed" or "was poured out on" the leaders of the Hebrew people and the prophets. It was this Spirit of which Ezekiel spoke:

I will sprinkle clean water upon you to cleanse you from all your impurities, and from all your idols I will cleanse you. I will give you a new heart and place a new spirit within you, taking from your bodies your stony hearts and giving you natural hearts. I will put my spirit within you and make you live by my statutes, careful to observe my decrees. You shall live in the land I gave your fathers; you shall be my people, and I will be your God.

(36:25-28)

And it was this Spirit which Joel prophesied would be given in the New Covenant, not just to the leaders, but to all the people:

Then afterward I will pour out
my spirit upon all mankind.
Your sons and daughters shall prophesy,
your old men shall dream dreams,
your young men shall see visions;

Even upon the servants and the handmaids,
   in those days, I will pour out my spirit.
And I will work wonders in the heavens
   and on the earth,
      blood, fire, and columns of smoke. . . .

(3:1-3)

The word used in the New Testament which is translated as "Spirit" is the Greek word *pneuma*. It means essentially the same thing as in the Old Testament. It is the Spirit of Yahweh, the Spirit of God, the Spirit of Jesus. Who is the Spirit? He is the life and love and power shared between the Father and the Son, the life and power of God Himself.

JESUS AND THE SPIRIT

Jesus was conceived by the power of the Spirit. After Jesus had grown up, He went out to the desert to hear his cousin John preach. All four Gospels recount the story of Jesus' baptism by John and of his receiving the Holy Spirit. This is to say that Jesus, the man, the carpenter, did not begin His ministry until the Spirit was manifested at John's baptism. John the Baptist said of Him, "I am baptizing you in water, but there is one to come who is mightier than I. I am not fit to loosen his sandal strap. He will baptize you in the Holy Spirit and in fire" (Luke 3:16). The new covenant which God would make with men would be to share His own life with them. In an older theological language we called it "sanctifying grace": the gift (grace) which makes us holy (sanctified); and as we have already seen, to be holy is to share in God's own life, His Spirit.

Luke goes on to say what effect the coming of the Holy Spirit had on Jesus: "Jesus, full of the Holy Spirit, then returned from the Jordan and was conducted by the Spirit into the desert. . ." (4:1). "Jesus returned in the power of the Spirit" (4:14) to Galilee.

He came to Nazareth where he had been reared, and entering the synagogue on the sabbath as he was in the habit of doing, he stood up to do the reading. When the book of the prophet Isaiah was handed him, he unrolled the scroll and found the passage where it was written:

"The spirit of the Lord is upon me;
    therefore he has anointed me.
He has sent me to bring glad tidings to the poor,
    to proclaim liberty to captives,
Recovery of sight to the blind
    and release to prisoners,
To announce a year of favor from the Lord."

Rolling up the scroll he gave it back to the assistant and sat down. All in the synagogue had their eyes fixed on him. Then he began by saying to them, "Today this Scripture passage is fulfilled in your hearing."

(4:16-21)

In reading Scripture or Pentecostal literature or the canons of the Mass, you come across phrases such as "full of the Spirit," "filled with the Spirit," "anointed by the Spirit," or "Spirit-filled." What happened to Jesus and what we shall soon see happened to the apostles and early Christians explain what these phrases mean. Specifically, they mean that the Messianic Age, the time of the New Covenant, has begun. It is the Age of the Spirit, first in the person of Jesus, then in His Body, the Church.

The Spirit manifests the presence and power and love of God in the Messiah, Jesus. Describing the works of Jesus is describing the work of the Holy Spirit. So, where the Spirit of God is, we expect the works of the Messianic Presence. Jesus spoke and taught with authority. He healed, drove out demons, prophesied, loved, called to repentance, forgave sins, spoke with wisdom and knowledge, lived in total obedience to the Father, lived in total trust of the Father, and shared His life with His followers. In subsequent chapters we want to explore in more detail how the Body of Christ, the Church, is meant to be the continuation of the Messianic Presence, and that, therefore, all the Messianic signs are meant to be present in it.

For now, let us remember that the same Spirit which Jesus received He promised to us. John tells us:

On the last and greatest day of the festival, Jesus stood up and cried out:
    "If anyone thirsts, let him come to me;

let him drink who believes in me.
Scripture has it:
'From within him rivers of living
water shall flow.' "

(Here he was referring to the Spirit, whom those that came to believe in him were to receive. There was, of course, no Spirit as yet, since Jesus had not yet been glorified)

(John 7:37-39)

THE SPIRIT AND THE APOSTLES

From John 14 through 17, Jesus comforts, teaches, encourages His apostles and prophesies about their future. He tells them that He and the Father will be with them, and He tells them that it is better that He go because He and the Father will send them the Holy Spirit who will teach them and comfort them and empower them. The Spirit, Jesus says, "will take what I give him and tell it to you." (16:15 — TEV)

Then, after the resurrection, Jesus tells the apostles, "Do not leave Jerusalem, but wait for the gift my Father promised, that I told you about. For John baptized with water, but in a few days you will be baptized with the Holy Spirit" (Acts 1:4-5 — TEV). And then: "You will receive power when the Holy Spirit comes down on you; then you are to be my witnesses in Jersusalem, throughout Judea and Samaria, yes, even to the ends of the earth" (1:8).

What is happening here is the unfolding of God's plan to renew the earth. He sent Jesus to reveal His love for us and to announce the Kingdom. The Messianic Presence was in Jesus but was confined in place and time to His person. Jesus passed on the Spirit to all of us so that the Messianic Presence might be in every place and all time, in His Body, His Church.

If you read the Acts of the Apostles (called in the early Church, "The Acts of the Spirit") and the Epistles, looking for the role of the Holy Spirit, it fairly jumps out of the page at you. Skim the New Testament and see. For our purposes here, we will draw attention only to a few instances. In his very first sermon, immediately after the first Pentecostal experience, Peter calls attention to the prophecy of Joel already cited above. This

117

is the beginning of the Age of the Spirit. When he has finished his sermon, the people ask Peter what they must do to be saved, and Peter replies: "Turn away from your sins, each one of you, and be baptized in the name of Jesus Christ, so that your sins will be forgiven; and you will receive God's gift, the Holy Spirit. For God's promise was made to you and your children, and to all who are far away — all whom the Lord our God calls to himself" (Acts 2:38-39 — TEV).

THE SPIRIT AND THE BELIEVER

Wherever the message is preached, reference is made to receiving the Holy Spirit, and what is especially important to note, *the effects of it were experienced.* The Spirit is given to empower, to manifest the presence and power and love of God. Miracles and wonders accompanied the preaching. People shared what they had with each other, they prayed together, and they shared the Lord's supper with each other.

When Paul preached, he gloried in his weakness so that it would be clear that the power came from God. In the beginning of his first letter to the Corinthians, he makes it plain that he did not attempt to preach with human wisdom so that our faith would not rest on human wisdom but on God's power, that is, His Spirit. And he claims that only those who have God's Spirit can understand the things of the Spirit, because to others the Gospel is scandal or foolishness. Paul takes for granted that his readers have *experienced* God's Spirit in their lives. In the beginning of his letter to the Ephesians he says, "The Spirit is the guarantee that we shall receive what God has promised his people, and assures us that God will give complete freedom to those who are his" (1:14 — TEV). "Guarantee" is a word which requires an experience on the part of his readers. In other words, those who have received the Spirit are expected to *know* that they have received it.

In Galatians, Paul writes:

> You senseless Galatians! Who has cast a spell over you — you before whose eyes Jesus Christ was displayed to view upon his cross? I want to learn only one thing from you: how did you receive the Spirit? Was it through

observance of the law or through faith in what you heard? How could you be so stupid? After beginning in the spirit, are you now to end in the flesh? Have you had such remarkable experiences all to no purpose — if indeed they were to no purpose? Is it because you observe the law or because you have faith in what you heard that God lavishes the Spirit on you and works wonders in your midst?

(Galatians 3:1-5)

Isn't it plain enough? God gives us His own Holy Spirit and through this wonderful gift reveals Himself to us in a tangible way and empowers us to be the Body of Christ, the Messianic Presence. We really should expect our life together to be full of the signs and wonders and manifestations of the Spirit who gives us life. We should expect the Spirit to guide us and teach us and comfort us.

All of this is happening among those who believe, and it will happen among us as each of us claims the power of the Spirit for himself. For those of us who are older, there is much that coincides with our earlier experience. In the forties and fifties people flocked to novenas and prayed for miracles and healings. People still make pilgrimages to shrines to ask for miracles and healings.

THE SPIRIT AND US

What is different today is expecting God to reveal Himself to us so that we might know Him and understand His Word, the Scriptures, and that we might claim His power in our lives. How much we can claim will be the material of the rest of this book. For now we concentrate on the power to know Him, love Him, to have the desire to pray, to experience the joy and peace He promises, to understand His word.

Why did this not just happen to us through the Sacraments of Baptism and Confirmation? Why is this something new? These are good questions and pertinent ones. I think that the answer is a simple one: we did not expect anything like this to happen to us. We weren't taught that we should expect it and, more importantly, it wasn't happening to anyone around us. It wasn't part of the taken-for-granted life of the parish.

119

Our understanding of the way God works through the sacraments has been tinged with a sense of the magical. That is not how theologians have explained the sacraments, but the popular practice has nevertheless been somewhat magical: go through the ritual and something will happen.

Being born into a Catholic family and baptized as an infant is being born into a community of faith. As the child grows, it is expected that he will absorb the faith of the community and gradually experience in himself the power and love of God. This requires a series of choices to accept the Lordship of Jesus. As his "self" develops, there are usually some significant moments in which he must choose his own way or God's Lordship. If he has grown up in a vital Christian community where God's presence and power are manifest and where the joy and peace of Christ is real, then he will be making thousands of little choices as he grows up; and then those especially significant ones will be fairly easy. For him there will be no outstanding experience of conversion, or of being "reborn," or of the "baptism of the Spirit." Instead of happening all at once, it will happen gradually.

On the other hand, for those of us who grew up in a church in which the faith was not powerfully alive, or who drifted away from the faith, a call to repentance and the acceptance of the fullness of the Spirit, requires a decision which is usually more dramatic. It is similar to the difference between falling in love gradually and falling in love suddenly.

If we look back to when we received the Sacrament of Confirmation, and recall the attitude we had then, I think it is easy to see why none of the things we've been talking about happened to us. We were prepared for the sacrament by being required to memorize questions and answers from a catechism. Part of the ritual was a "test." Another part of the ritual involved the bishop slapping us on the face. What was going through your mind as you sat there in church during the ceremony? Did you expect to receive the gift of tongues or prophecy or the power to witness? Or were you wondering, as I was, whether or not you would remember the answers to the questions, and how hard was the bishop going to slap you, and what presents were you going to receive?

EXPERIENCING THE SPIRIT

Since we didn't approach the sacrament with expectant faith, the power of the Spirit was not released. Of course, we did receive the Spirit, but He can only act where we claim His power in faith. In this and subsequent chapters we are calling you to claim the power you already have. You have the Spirit of God in you. He wishes to manifest Himself to the world through you. It is up to you to claim it!

Does God seem to be far away and not at all interested in you? Call on the Spirit within you to reveal your Father to you. In the eighth chapter of Romans, Paul says:

> All who are led by the Spirit of God are sons of God. You did not receive a spirit of slavery leading you back into fear, but a spirit of adoption through which we cry out, "Abba!" (that is, "Father").
> (14-15)
> But if we are children, we are heirs as well: heirs of God, heirs with Christ, if only we suffer with him so as to be glorified with him. (17)

Have you felt yourself lacking the strength or power to be what you know God wants you to be and what you would really like to be? Ask God for that power. Ask Jesus to pour out His Spirit on you, to release in you the power of His Spirit. Read and meditate on Ephesians 3:14-21. Ask the Spirit to give you understanding.

In subsequent chapters we will talk about the gifts and ministries of the Spirit for the Church and of how these are connected with the organizational aspects of the Church. For now, simply pray for the release of the Spirit in your own life. Our Father is a good Father, a Father who loves us. Jesus is the Good Shepherd who loved us enough to die for us and who loves us enough to share His Spirit with us. Expect Him to work in you.

As you pray to Jesus for the release of the Spirit, expect: (1) the experience of God's presence and love, (2) a simple

121

expectant faith, (3) power to understand Scripture, (4) the power to pray and a hunger for prayer, and (5) the peace and joy which comes from knowing God.

THE GIFT OF TONGUES

We want to give special attention at this point to the gift of tongues, not because it is extremely important in itself, but because it seems to be a stumbling block for some. The gift of tongues is valuable, of course, because it is one of the gifts which God gives. That is enough to make it important. For some it has the additional dimension of being an obstacle: they do not want it. So we deal with it here. If the amount of space we give it seems out of proportion, that is only because it is the least understood gift and therefore most in need of explanation.

Let it be said right at the beginning that God does not give the gift of tongues to everyone, and, further, that the sign of the fullness of the Spirit is not to be equated with speaking in tongues. "Classic" Pentecostals have made that equation a dogma ever since Charles Fox Parham began teaching and preaching, but it has never been accepted by any of the historic mainline churches. There are two very good reasons for not accepting the equation: (1) the Scripture on which such an interpretation is based can be interpreted in other ways, and (2) experience shows so very clearly that the Spirit works powerfully in many people who do not have the gift of tongues.

So, it should be clear that you do not need to speak in tongues in order to be filled with the Spirit. Or, to put that another way, if you do not speak in tongues, that is not a sign that you have not yielded to the Spirit in your life.

A TURNING POINT

Still, there is something to be said about urging people to expect the gift of tongues and of instructing them on how it might be received. The value in such an approach lies in the presentation of the choice to be open to whatever God wants to give. The choice to accept tongues is for many Americans a kind of "bridge-burning" event.

It amounts to the choice to accept a new sign of

identification: "Yes, I do speak in tongues," or "Yes, I am one of those who speak in tongues." For a variety of reasons, some people are reluctant to accept this gift from God, and the presentation of this choice brings that out. If we are to be open to whatever God wants, then we must be open even to that gift which might seem strange to our family or friends. If the reasons for not wanting what God offers are brought to light, then they can be dealt with by teaching or repentance or healing.

Sometimes the reason for not wanting the gift is a sense of doing something foolish and embarrassing. At least two things are involved here. One is a misunderstanding; the other is a lack of freedom to be foolish. The latter is a hindrance in doing almost anything well and is a sign of a lack of self-confidence (among other things). A return to childlike simplicity and wonder in an environment of creative, loving people can be the healing of such fear. The misunderstanding, which is inhibiting, is corrected by teaching, teaching which shows that speaking in tongues is not foolish at all, but a beautiful and effective form of prayer. We will develop this later.

Another reason for not wanting the gift of tongues is that some people claim that speaking in tongues is a symptom of psychological disturbance, or, at least, that it is only incoherent babbling. Sometimes studies are cited to back this up. I really do not feel a need to go into detail in dealing with this objection. First of all, it is not a common problem. Second, many others have already dealt adequately with the problem, men like McDonnell, Kelsey, Sherrill, Gelpi, and O'Connor (see the bibliography). Thirdly, my own experience and the experience of thousands of others completely contradicts that kind of theorizing.

Still another reason for not wanting the gift of tongues is the usual reluctance to try something one has not tried before. Someone said to me the other day that we need to pull ourselves up out of our ruts every now and then, just to look around and see what else is happening in the world. We nestle in our ruts. They are familiar. We can be complacent there. It is so easy to say: "I go to church on Sunday, and I do what I am supposed to do. I don't need any of that new stuff." An obvious problem with the gift of tongues is the absence of any felt need for it. If I have not yet experienced something, then I cannot say for myself that it is good or bad. I can only rely on the testimony of others.

GIFT OF PERSONAL PRAYER

So, what do others say? The gift of tongues was presented to me as a gift of prayer, as a new Spirit-inspired language of praise, as a way in which the Spirit takes over our power of speech and speaks perfect prayers to the Father for us. My own experience with it has been a good one. Praying in tongues helps me to open my spirit to God's Spirit in prayer. I find it easier to come into recollectedness and a prayerful spirit when I begin by praying in tongues. I also find it relaxing and joyful to pray and sing in tongues with my mind on the presence of the Lord. I almost always break into a smile for no apparent reason as I pray quietly in tongues to myself. I also find it useful to pray in tongues when I don't know what to pray for or when I run out of ways of praising the Lord. So often people ask me to pray for them or for some situation and I just don't know what the Lord wants, so I pray in tongues. These are the same things that I find others saying about their experience with this beautiful gift.

From all this it should be apparent that the gift of tongues is primarily a gift for use in personal prayer. In conjunction with the gift of interpretation, it may be used prophetically in group prayer or even alone; but we treat this in the next chapter. Here we are describing its use as a speech and song gift for personal prayer. This is the really important thing to grasp here: God gives this gift to you for your own use in personal prayer. Paul explains this in Romans:

> The Spirit too helps us in our weakness, for we do not know how to pray as we ought; but the Spirit himself makes intercession for us with groanings that cannot be expressed in speech. He who searches hearts knows what the Spirit means, for the Spirit intercedes for the saints as God himself wills.

> (8:26)

In I Corinthians 12-14 Paul is primarily giving an instruction about the prayer meetings in Corinth, but he does make these remarks about the gift of tongues: "A man who speaks in a tongue is talking not to men but to God. No one understands him, because he utters mysteries in the Spirit" (14:2). "He who speaks in a tongue builds up himself..." (4). These are important things to take to heart. Praying in tongues is speaking to God, and through it one is built up. In this whole section Paul is urging the Corinthians not to use the gift of tongues without interpretation *at public meetings*. That is why he says:

> If I pray in a tongue my spirit is at prayer but my mind contributes nothing. What is my point here? I want to pray with my spirit, and also to pray with my mind. I want to sing with my spirit and with my mind as well. If your praise of God is solely with the spirit, how will the one who does not comprehend be able to say "Amen" to your thanksgiving? He will not know what you are saying. You will be uttering praise very well indeed, but the other man will not be helped. Thank God, I speak in tongues more than any of you, but in church I would rather say five intelligible words to instruct others than ten thousand words in a tongue.
>
> (13-19)

Notice how powerfully Paul speaks of the private use of the gift. He wants to pray and sing in the Spirit: "You will be uttering praise very well indeed...." And he thanks God that he speaks in tongues more than anyone else. The point I am trying to make here is that this gift is far from being foolish and an embarrassment. It is a beautiful gift of prayer, good for being built up by the Spirit. God knows we need it, so He gives it to us.

Notice, too, that Paul wants us to pray *both* in the Spirit and with our minds. In Ephesians he says: "At every opportunity pray in the Spirit, using prayers and petitions of every sort" (6:18). When we pray in tongues we do not understand what we are saying. It is the Spirit who prays in us. But we should also follow the leading of the Spirit in those prayers which we do understand, the prayers which the Lord

125

puts in our hearts, the ones we say in our own language. It is not a case of either/or, but of both/and.

WORDLESS COMMUNION

The fact that we do not understand what we say in tongues is not an obstacle; it is a blessing. The deepest communication is speechless, beyond our power to verbalize. Our bodies speak it; our hearts speak it; our spirit speaks it; a word is often even an intrusion on the sacredness of communion. Many of us have lost or never learned to communicate at this level. We are satisfied to play with superficial clever or gossipy conversations. We have forgotten the childlike experience of being lost in wonder, of just *being with* another. We have forgotten how good it is to be so lost in the wonder of another or of some magnificent thing that our communication and our prayer are impoverished. Enter into the Holy, into the Sacred Presence of God in prayer and know what a great joy it is to let the Spirit give you speech.

The gift of tongues is a beautiful and sacred gift of God. We should pray for it with faith and hope. Most receive it just for the asking. Sometimes, though, someone asks for the gift and God says No. If that is the case, there are several things to do. First, an examination of conscience is in order. Is there any obstacle in your relationship with Jesus, in your relationship with your neighbor, any lack of forgiveness? God's withholding of the gift may be intended to bring this to your mind so that you may repent. If so, repent and ask again.

If your conscience is clear, then ask for others to pray with you. The prayer of brothers and sisters together reminds us of our unity in the Body of Christ, and sometimes God grants the gift in these circumstances just to remind us of that.

If that doesn't work, then remember that the gift of tongues is a gift. It is not a reward. It is freely given. It has nothing to do with your level of sanctity, but only of God's choice. I know several people whom the Lord uses powerfully in teaching who do not speak in tongues. And, I remember praying with a large group of Sisters in Mississippi some years ago for the gift of tongues. One Dominican Sister was praying with us for the rest and all those she prayed for received the gift, but she never did.

The Spirit worked in her and through her in a beautiful and powerful way, but she never received the gift of tongues. Some don't. That is not a stigma.

RECEIVING THE GIFT OF TONGUES

Step 1. To receive the gift of tongues, begin by relaxing. It is not something you can do for yourself, so there is no point in becoming all worked up trying to get it. You don't get it, you *receive* it. Find the most relaxing place and position you can. One person I know received it in the bathtub!

Step 2. Enter into God's presence. Focus your attention on the presence of Jesus, the giver of the gift. We do not baptize in the Spirit. We do not give the gifts. Jesus does. Focus on His presence. Remember His perfect love for you.

Step 3. Ask Him to stir up the Spirit within you, to pour out His Spirit upon you, to fill you up so that it rushes out of you in this new language of prayer.

Step 4. Open your mouth and speak out, your mind and heart on Him. Speak out in anything but your native language. Let the Spirit form the language, the syllables. Praise Him.

If after a few minutes Jesus has not given you this gift, switch to English and talk to Him. Be silent for a while. Talk to Him again and try again. Be persevering, but don't be excessive. If you don't receive it, try again another time and follow the advice we gave above.

Praise God, the giver of all good gifts!

BIBLIOGRAPHY

RECOMMENDED READING:

Bittlinger, Arnold, and McDonnell, Kilian, OSB, *The Baptism in the Holy Spirit as an Ecumenical Problem* (Two essays relating the Baptism in the Holy Spirit to the Sacramental life), Charismatic Renewal Services, Notre Dame, Indiana, 1972, 53pp.

Excellent for connecting the Pentecostal experience to a broader, more traditional theology.

Clark, Stephen, *Baptized in the Spirit,* Dove Publications, Pecos, New Mexico, 1970, 76pp.

A simple and clear explanation of the experience from the Catholic point of view.

Lange, Joseph, OSFS, *The Weber Lectures,* 1972, 24pp.

Paper delivered at Moravian Theological Seminary on the relationship of the charismatic ministry to the institutional church.

Haughey, John C., SJ, *The Conspiracy of God: The Holy Spirit in Men,* Doubleday, Garden City, N.Y., 1973, 154pp.

Great for understanding the person of the Holy Spirit. Especially good in relating the Spirit to the mission of Jesus. Cardinal Suenens called it "the best book in English I have read on the Holy Spirit in recent years."

Ranaghan, Dorothy and Kevin, *Catholic Pentecostals,* Paulist Press, New York, N.Y., 1969, 266pp.

Basic instruction in the history and theology of the Charismatic Renewal. Especially good for the personal witness of those who were involved in the beginning of the movement.

SUPPLEMENTARY READING:

Harper, Michael, *Power for the Body of Christ,* Fountain Trust, London, 1964, 55pp.

One of the best introductory books on the work of the Spirit — clear, direct and helpful.

Sherrill, John, *They Speak with Other Tongues,* Fleming H. Revell Co., Old Tappan, N.J., 1965, 140pp.

The story of a skeptical reporter's investigations into the gift of tongues and how he overcame his doubts to experience the Spirit in this gift.

by Tony Cushing

Charismatic Prayer 8

When I was a child, the most impressive things about the Catholic faith were the devotions to Mary and the Blessed Sacrament. May devotions used to bring five or six hundred people together to sing and pray the rosary. It just seemed right to be there — warm from praying, cool from the marble of the church, singing "Hail, Holy Queen" and meaning it. Benediction was much more awesome. Mary was a comfortable person to be with, but Jesus, well, even the priest knew that this was the untouchable God. Again, singing and praising God in the Litany of the Saints was a very right thing to do. You felt the reverence and the mystery.

My sense of the presence of God crystallized even more when I visited the shrine of St. Anne de Beaupre. My mother had cancer, and we were going to ask God to cure her at the shrine. We found an atmosphere of expectancy there which was unlike anything else. The whole town was holy (they wouldn't even sell beer to my uncle). The vestibule of the church was filled with the crutches, wheel chairs and eye glasses of those who had been cured. Seeing that, you really expected God to do something special. And the thousands in the candlelight processions, the women praying their way up the steps on their knees, the groups at the stations — you knew that here was a special place where even ordinary people could be touched by God.

Well, Vatican II came along (at a time when I no longer cared about devotions) and changed a lot of our prayer forms. These old devotions didn't seem to fit in with the modern world; suddenly many Catholics were deprived of them. Even in the convents, action started replacing public prayer as the thing Catholics should do together. Regrettably, in the transition after the Council no new forms of public prayer sprang up to replace the vanished devotions. Gradually, however, the people who wanted and needed prayer discovered new approaches to worship. One of these prayer forms is charismatic prayer.

There are various types of common prayer, and each one has its own dynamics or style. The reason for this is that different groups have their own special "something" which takes place when the group meets. The "something" that goes on among close friends is much different from the "something" at a large party or a football game. What is different about each group is the kind of relationship shared among the people. The old friends have years of shared experience and ideas which creates an intense intimacy. But at a football game the most everyone has in common is watching the game. Any group in prayer, and especially a charismatic group, believes that the "something" they share is a relationship with Jesus and the Father and the experience of the Holy Spirit.

Another element which distinguishes various forms of prayer is the common expectation of what God will do when we come together. The people at the shrine had the kind of faith that expected God to do a lot for them. May devotions were quite different, and if someone was cured there, there would have been a lot of fainting. Well, charismatic prayer calls people to that kind of expectant faith which says that God is going to touch us, speak to us and heal us.

At a large charismatic prayer meeting there are many different kinds of people, at many different levels of spirituality. The "something" they have in common is a shared experience of Jesus and a mutual desire to witness and celebrate the presence of Jesus among them. The people there might not even know each other well. It really isn't that necessary that they do (though it helps). This is because they are there to celebrate

Emmanuel — "God with us." So they rejoice and respond to the God who *is* with us by praising Him and thanking Him. That is what the word *Alleluia!* is all about.

In describing what a charismatic meeting is like, I would say that two things stand out: spontaneous praise and the belief in the inspiration of the Holy Spirit expressing itself in the charisms or gifts. There is little structuring, and the form of the meeting usually has an organic order which varies with each group. Generally, in the different meetings I've been to, there is a period of song and spontaneous praise at the beginning of the meeting. This lasts as long as the people feel inspired to keep it going — sometimes in our group it's lasted for the entire meeting. As the group focuses more and more on the presence of God, a few people might be inspired to read a passage from Scripture or to share some experience (like an answered prayer) or insight that they had during the week. Others might be inspired to prophesy (speak in the first person a message or inspiration from the Holy Spirit). Still others might feel led to teach about a certain aspect of the Gospel or to exhort or encourage people to a bolder faith or deeper love. These charisms or manifestations of the Holy Spirit are intended to increase the faith and love of the entire group. And all of this is done in a spontaneous way. The meeting is led by the Holy Spirit who inspires and instructs the group as they respond to Him in prayer.

There is a kind of two-fold action of praising God and hearing and responding to His word. Often I think this takes on the same dynamics as the Mass: repentance, praise, hearing the word, recognizing and responding to Christ's presence, and being sent forth to serve. I guess it's just natural for the Spirit to work that way in Catholics.

For most Catholics it is a very unfamiliar way of communicating with God. And because it is different, some people experience a sort of cultural shock. The same kind of thing happens when Americans visit Mexico. The Mexicans speak to you with their face six inches from yours (we prefer a two to three foot distance). Most Americans, on experiencing this novel style of communication, feel at least uncomfortable and often downright threatened. Of course, some Americans feel right at home doing this. Well it's the same with charismatic prayer. Initial reactions vary from "It's beautiful" to "It's weird," depending on the person's background. Most people, though, are impressed by the sincerity and warmth and joy of the meetings.

What I want to do now is to go through these various elements of charismatic prayer and describe how we've experienced them and what their value and function is in community. Hopefully I'll be able to tie this in to some of the more traditional practices of worship among Catholics.

EXPERIENCING GOD

Charismatic prayer involves experiencing the presense and the power of God in our midst. This is possible because the Holy Spirit dwells within us and fills the hearts of the faithful and kindles in them the fire of divine love. If we look at Pentecost, we see that something definitely happens when people pray for and receive the Spirit: "They began to express themselves in foreign tongues and make bold proclamation as the Spirit prompted them. Staying in Jerusalem at the time were devout Jews of every nation under heaven. These heard the sound, and assembled in a large crowd" (Acts 2:4-6).

And their reaction is noteworthy: "The whole occurrence astonished them. They asked in utter amazement, ... they were dumbfounded and could make nothing at all of what had happened. 'What does this mean?' they asked one another, while a few remarked with a sneer, 'They have had too much new wine' " (Acts 2:7, 12, 13). One gets the impression that something physical happened to the apostles. They were speaking in tongues and seemed so excited about the way they experienced the presence of God that the racket of praise they made drew a huge crowd.

It seems that prayer was a joyful experience. Being in the presence of God made these people happy — it made a difference. It was also baffling to those gathered outside. If this scene appears too emotional, take a look at the Psalms:

Sing joyfully to the Lord, all you lands;
  serve the Lord with gladness;

come before him with joyful song . . .
Enter his gates with thanksgiving,
   his courts with praise;
Give thanks to him; bless his name, for he is good. . . .
                       (Psalm 100: 1, 2, 4, 5)

Therefore my heart is glad and my soul rejoices,
   my body, too, abides in confidence . . .
You will show me the path to life,
   fullness of joys in your presence,
   the delights at your right hand forever.
                       (Psalm 16: 9, 11)

O Lord, in your strength the king is glad;
   in your victory how greatly he rejoices . . .
   you gladdened him with the joy of your presence.
                       (Psalm 21: 2, 7)

And I will offer in his tent
   sacrifices with shouts of gladness;
I will sing and chant praise to the Lord . . .
   your presence, Lord, I seek.
                       (Psalm 27:6, 8)

A HUMAN RESPONSE

At least on occasion we are supposed to enjoy the presence
of God. This can invlove emotions. In three years of charismatic
prayer meetings, I've seen nearly every aspect of our relationship
with God displayed. Sometimes people get so happy about what
God has done for them that they laugh a lot. Once in a while
there is a general feeling of unworthiness and repentance which
a few people may express by crying. At other times the presence
of God has been such an awesome reality that the whole group
has spontaneously knelt down in a profound adoration. This is
to say that we can love, worship and experience God with the
emotions He gave us. There is nothing wrong about being
emotional in our love of God as long as we realize that this is
neither the goal nor the entirety of religion.

133

Back in the middle ages it was a common occurrence to see people kneeling at a roadside shrine weeping for their sins. It's just that American religion has so down-played emotion that being pious now has the connotation of being a sour-puss. Yet these same Americans will work themselves into a frenzy whenever somebody called a halfback carries an inflated pigskin past eleven men who are trying to knock him down. Don't get me wrong, I do the same thing. But somehow the idea has gotten around that to express emotions is to deny rationality. In college I used to see professors of physics and mathematics get absolutely ecstatic about solving a knotty problem. People are "fanatics" and "holy rollers," however, if they clap when singing or lift up their hands in praise of God. Yet you can groan, contract, and writhe when dancing to a rock band (again, I do it also). This reminds me of the legend that St. Francis got so excited while talking about God's love that he started to do a tap dance in joy. The point here is that we're just not used to getting emotional about the love of God. It's not part of our culture. Doesn't it make sense that if you can get wild about football, maybe you should get excited about praying to the God who loves you, forgives you, and gives your whole life meaning.

It's important to remember that joy and peace are results or by-products of focusing on Jesus. You don't come to prayer to "feel good." You come to seek God and encounter Him, and that *can* make you feel good. This is the normal dynamics of relationships. If you go up to someone and say, "Make me laugh," chances are he'll end up boring you. That's because your attention is on yourself. But if you concentrate on the other person, you probably will feel better and may even share a few laughs.

The key to all of this is an expectant faith. We need to believe that God wants us to praise Him, believe that He really will be present to us, expect that His spirit will work in us, believe that He answers our prayers and does speak to us. We need the faith to pray like the apostles: "Stretch out your hand to heal, and grant that wonders and miracles may be performed through the name of your holy Servant Jesus" (Acts 4:30 — TEV).

PRAISE FOR A LOVING GOD

There are all kinds of communal prayer — the Divine Office, Benediction, the rosary, conversational prayer, the Eucharist. Each has a particular emphasis or style. The particular emphasis of charismatic prayer is a very exuberant vocal praise. But, what is praise? I think of praise as recognizing God for how good and loving He is. You express your love to Him. You show how much you appreciate God. We do it all the time in the Mass. Especially after we repent of our sins and accept His forgiveness, the priest says, "Let us praise the glorious God." We respond, "Glory to God in the highest. We praise you, we bless you, we worship you, we give you thanks for your great glory." The book of Revelation contains beautiful passages of praise:

> Lord, God Almighty,
> How great and wonderful are your deeds!
> King of all nations,
> How right and true are your ways!
> Who will not fear you, Lord?
> Who will refuse to declare your greatness?
>
> (Revelation 15:3, 4 — TEV)

> Our Lord and God! You are worthy
> To receive glory and honor, and power.
> For you created all things,
> And by your will they were given existence and life.
>
> (Revelation 4:11 — TEV)

We praise Him because we know who He is, and He deserves to be praised. It is the praise of the lover for the beloved. Lovers are aware of their unworthiness and rejoice in the gift of love. Lovers rejoice in being loved by someone as great as their beloved. So we praise God for His goodness. Praise Him for His holiness and His greatness. Praise Him for His mercy. Praise Him for His beauty. Praise Him for His kindness. And most of all, praise Him for His love.

135

And we praise and thank Him for what He's done for us:
Bless the Lord, O my soul,
    and forget not all his benefits;
He pardons all your iniquities,
    he heals all your ills.

(Psalm 103:2, 3)

So we thank God for having died for us. Thank Him for forgiving us. Thank Him for sending His Spirit. Thank Him for calling us together. Thank Him for His gifts. Thank Him for revealing Himself to us. Thank Him for health, for sunshine and a spring day. Thank Him for everything and anything. This is all very orthodox and traditional. What is different is doing it spontaneously, aloud and together. It's like each one saying his own unique *gloria,* all at the same time. Where traditional worship is like a Mozart concerto, charismatic prayer is like a jazz festival. It's a question of participation.

Why praise God together? Can't we praise God in the privacy of our own rooms? The answer is that we should praise God privately *and* together. Communal prayer is somehow "more excellent" than private prayer. The reason for this is the witness of group prayer. Christianity happens in the context of a loving community. This community needs to show its love and worship to the world so that the people of the world will believe that the Father loves them as He loves Jesus (John 17:21). Community prayer makes a demonstration of our love for God.

"You, however, are 'a chosen race, a royal priesthood, a holy nation, a people he claims for his own to proclaim the glorious works of the One who called you from darkness into His marvelous light' " (1 Peter 2:9). The world needs to see people who really want to praise God, who *enjoy* praising God. Sometimes people have come to our prayer meetings as convinced skeptics. During the course of the meeting, they really experience God in a new way, confessing, "God is truly among you" (I Corinthians 14:25). Many devout people learn to pray in a new and richer way. There was one priest, the principal of an area high school who went to a meeting "just to find out what goes on." He felt very uncomfortable at first; but as he started to pray, he said he "felt more in the spirit of things" and he eventually prayed in tongues and came out "very renewed in his faith." What happened was that he encountered a group of people who had faith in the Spirit working among them — so through them his faith was re-charged.

Group prayer is where we witness or demonstrate to each other what God is doing in our lives. Just to hear everyone praying aloud often convinces me that these people really do love God. Our praising God increases our faith. We pray first for the Lord. Secondly, however, our very prayer is a gift to "build up the community." One night I went to our open prayer meeting feeling very bored. It just so happened that I sat next to a man who was there for the first night, who took very seriously our suggestion to participate and pray out loud. He just talked to Jesus, saying things like "Thank you, Lord, for still caring about me. Jesus, I haven't talked to You in ten years; it's really good now to be with You. Lord, teach me how to love You; I don't know, I'm so weak." Well, this man's sincerity really humbled me. The more he prayed, the more I was able to join with him in an honest repentance.

This leads us to another value of this kind of group prayer. Just by coming together we are in some way repenting. Even though spontaneity in following the Spirit is cherished, we do not come to do our own thing in prayer. We come to do the Spirit's thing, so He works in the unity of the whole community. We pray as the Body of Christ united. Practically, this means that we choose to do what the Spirit leads the group to do. This choice is above our moods and feelings. If we don't feel like singing when we come, we choose to follow Jesus as He's leading the whole group in song. This means that sometimes there is some effort entailed. We might not always want to pray or sing or be silent as the group is doing, so we choose to do what we consider to be important and ignore our feelings. This in itself is a kind of repentance — a giving up of our wills to God.

And what usually happens is that, as we choose to participate, our "feelings" will come around. This is not hypocrisy, but a conscious choice. Neither is this the purest form of prayer, but as G. K. Chesterton said, "Whatever is worth doing is worth doing poorly."

We usually understand this simply as getting the right priorities on why we come together to pray: 1) God, 2) others 3) self. Our desire is first to praise God, secondly to serve others, and thirdly to be filled ourselves. This is obviously the ideal. Most -of the time people come to prayer meetings to fill their own needs. That's okay and it's definitely something God wants to do. But if this attitude continues too long, most people will find that they are getting nothing out of the meetings. God wants them to start coming for His sake and for the service of others. When that happens and our focus is on Jesus, we find our needs fulfilled. This is merely applying to prayer meetings the Gospel commands of: "Seek first his Kingship over you, his way of holiness, and all these things will be given you besides" (Matthew 6:33) and ". . . whoever loses his life for my sake will find it" (Matthew 16:25).

When people come together to praise God and be inspired by His Holy Spirit to serve, we found that their faith needs are met. The prayer meeting is a way we learn to be closer to God. We also found that people are healed physically and psychologically through this "convincing power of the Spirit" (I Corinthians 2:4). The basic way this happens is through the gifts or charisms of the Holy Spirit (read and meditate on I Corinthians 12-14). But before I talk about how these gifts work in a prayer meeting, I'll have to deal generally with what they are and what their purpose is.

THE GIFTS OF THE SPIRIT

Most Catholics remember the gifts of the Spirit as mentioned in their confirmation — wisdom, counsel, knowledge, fortitude, piety, understanding and fear of the Lord, (used in Isaiah 11:2, 3 as a description of the Messiah). I would risk saying, without statistics, that most Catholics do not experience these as charism-gifts. Even if they do, it's not usually connected with the Sacrament of Confirmation, which gives us the power to become witnesses to Jesus. Well then, what are these charisms of the Spirit? St. Paul describes them this way:

> There are different gifts but the same Spirit; there are different ministries but the same Lord; there are different works but the same God who accomplishes all of them in everyone.
>
> (I Corinthians 12:4-6)

Generally we understand this to be any service done for the Lord whose source is the power of the Holy Spirit. The different ways the Spirit works include anything from ordinary housework and giving money to extraordinary things like healing and speaking in tongues.

> Allotting His gifts "to everyone according as he will" (I Cor. 12:11), He distributes special graces among the faithful of every rank. By these gifts He makes them fit and ready to undertake the various tasks or offices advantageous for the renewal and upbuilding of the Church ... "The manifestation of the Spirit is given to everyone for profit" (I Cor. 12:7). These charismatic gifts, whether they are the most outstanding or the more simple and widely diffused, are to be received with thanksgiving and consolation, for they are exceedingly suitable and useful for the needs of the Church.
>
> (Vatican II, *Dogmatic Constitution in the Church*, art. 12)

What is the purpose of these gifts? Paul says, "To each person the manifestation of the Spirit is given for the common good" (I Cor. 12:7). These gifts are tools or instruments to increase the faith, love and unity of the Christian community. They are ways of expressing our love of God and neighbor in an act of service. Their value is in glorifying Jesus ("And no one can say: 'Jesus is Lord,' except in the Holy Spirit" — I Cor. 12:3) and in building up or edifying the life of His Body — the church community. These gifts are means. If you're Catholic, it helps to think of these gifts as actual graces or inspirations: God doing something to lead you closer to Him (actual grace). It does not mean that you are holy or living in sanctifying grace (indwelling of the Holy Spirit). All it means is that God is doing

139

something to lead you closer to Him, whether you're holy or not. I try to think of spiritual gifts in the same way I would think of a shovel or a hammer. The value of a hammer is not in how nice it looks or that it is *my* hammer. The only real value of a tool is in how well it fulfills its purpose.

Paul indicates that the purpose of the charisms is love. "There are in the end three things that last: faith, hope, and love, and the greatest of these is love" (I Cor. 13:13). Love is essential. It is love that saves. It is God who is love (I John 4:8). To love is to be filled with the Holy Spirit of love. Even martyrdom is useless to help me if I don't have love (I Cor. 13:3).

This does not mean that the gifts are useless. It is not a question of either/or but of both/and. The gifts are not essential, but Paul saw value in them: "Set your hearts on the greater gifts" (I Cor. 12:31). In other words, if you want to drive a nail, it helps if you have the right tool. You can use a rock or try to use your hand, but it's an advantage to have a hammer designed for that purpose. God has designed gifts to help us love. It just makes sense to use what God wants to give.

What are these gifts? Well, Paul never gives a representative list. There are "different gifts" and "different ministries." He mentions preaching with wisdom, knowledge, faith, healing, miracles, prophecy, discernment (or recognizing spirits), speaking in tongues, ability to interpret tongues, teaching, helping, good leadership, apostleship (I Cor. 12:8-11, 28); giving away material possessions and martyrdom (I Cor. 13:3); marriage, and celibacy (I Cor. 7:7); administration, giving alms, doing works of mercy (Romans 12:6-8); evangelism (Eph. 4:11).

These were some of the ways in which the early communities experienced the power of the Spirit working miracles among them (Gal. 3:5). These are not the only ways God works, but "each one has his own gift from God, one this and another that" (I Cor. 7:7). It doesn't matter so much what a gift is as that it glorifies Jesus and builds up the community in love.

CHARISMS IN THE PRAYER MEETING

Now, to get back to prayer meetings, there are gifts given to build up the community in worship and love. Because of the limitations of the prayer meeting, these gifts usually aren't administration, martyrdom, almsgiving or things like that. What does happen is that the Spirit inspires people to pray, sing, witness, teach, etc.: contributions which enliven a prayer meeting. Paul writes:

> I continually thank my God for you because of the favor he has bestowed on you in Christ Jesus, in whom you have been richly endowed with every gift of speech and knowledge. Likewise, the witness I bore to Christ has been so confirmed among you that you lack no spiritual gift as you wait for the revelation of our Lord Jesus Christ.
>
> (I Cor. 1:4-7)

> Let the word of Christ, rich as it is, dwell in you. In wisdom made perfect, instruct and admonish one another. Sing gratefully to God from your hearts in psalms, hymns, and inspired songs. Whatever you do, whether in speech or in action, do it in the name of the Lord Jesus. Give thanks to God the Father through him.
>
> (Colossians 3:16, 17)

Prayer is the work of the Spirit. The kind of spontaneous praise and thanks I talked about earlier is an especially demonstrable Spirit-inspired prayer. Even singing hymns is seen as a gift of the Spirit. "Inspired song" is something I'll have to take some time to describe.

The footnote to Colossians 3:16 in *The Jerusalem Bible* expresses the opinion that "These 'inspired songs' could be charismatic improvisations suggested by the Spirit during liturgical assembly; cf. I Co. 12:7 f; 14:28." This is basically the way we have experienced this gift. In prayer the Spirit inspires a person or the group to sing in free-form melody and lyrics. The lyric-prayer could be in English or in tongues (a gift of praying in other languages). Each person sings his own unique song as the Spirit leads, and most of the time it harmonizes beautifully. It is a spontaneous chant of praise.

The first time I heard this was at what I thought was a "normal" prayer meeting. I didn't even know what the word "charismatic" meant. Anyway, people were thanking Jesus in a familiar way when suddenly they started this inspired singing. My reaction was something like, "That's nice: it's open, unlimited communication, like singing on a spring day. Lord, I want to do that." So I started singing, "Alleluia!" And then I started singing something else. It was all very peaceful and pleasant. It just seemed like a natural development. A few days later someone asked me if I ever prayed in tongues, and I didn't know what he meant.

Strange as it might sound, we found that this "singing in the Spirit" has touched a lot of people who were skeptical about the gifts of the Spirit. I remember a music director who was on a retreat with us. One night the whole group started singing in the Spirit. He was amazed that we had been singing "contrapuntal harmonies in a fugal mode" without a director, with our eyes closed and everyone stopping at the same time. This convinced him that we weren't just "acting pious" but that there was a divine element present.

There are many other ways in which the Spirit inspires prayer to build up the whole community. One person may pray aloud for the whole group in a kind of psalm of praise. Sometimes someone will ask God for a favor which holds meaning for the whole group, and it really touches people to have faith to accept what God gives. I can remember praying for the peace and joy of God's love to touch us in a special way. Afterwards someone told me that he had really worried about a problem, but that the way I prayed had a certain power or effect that helped him to experience what I had asked for. This has nothing to do with poetic ability or psychological insights (though God can use these things too) but rests on the "convincing power of the Spirit" (I Cor. 2:5).

> The Spirit too helps us in our weakness, for we do not
> know how to pray as we ought; but the Spirit himself

makes intercession for us with groanings which cannot be expressed in speech. He who searches hearts knows what the Spirit means, for the Spirit intercedes for the saints as God himself wills.

(Romans 8:26, 27)

PROPHECY

Prayer is also *listening* to God. The primary ways we hear God at a charismatic meeting are through the gifts of prophecy, wisdom, knowledge, and teaching. I want to go into detail to explain the gift of prophecy: what it is, how to use it and discern it, and what its value is. I start with prophecy because it is the most unusual and most valuable gift experienced in charismatic prayer. Also, everything I say about prophecy and how to use it will generally apply to the other gifts: I won't have to repeat myself. The value and proper use of these gifts are discussed in Chapter 14 of the first letter to the Corinthians. Paul begins: "Seek eagerly after love. Set your hearts on spiritual gifts — above all, the gift of prophecy" (I Cor. 14:1).

The reason for this is that the Corinthians were dazzled by the gift of tongues. Being more spectacular, it seemed more spiritual. But for Paul the gift of praying in tongues is chiefly for yourself: you talk in the Spirit about mysterious matters (I Cor. 14:2). This benefits the individual, or else how could Paul declare, "Thank God, I speak in tongues more than any of you" (I Cor. 14:18) and "...do not forbid those who speak in tongues..." (I Cor. 14:39)? In gatherings for worship another consideration becomes uppermost, however: "...but in the church I would rather say five intelligible words to instruct others than ten thousand words in a tongue" (I Cor. 14:19). The key here is what gifts are of value for the community.

So Paul, with the perception that love is what's essential, is free to encourage the proper use of all the gifts. If you are loving, then you'll use your gifts for the good of everybody. "I should like it if all of you spoke in tongues, but I much prefer that you prophesy. The prophet is greater than one who speaks in tongues..." (I Cor. 14:5). "The prophet ... speaks to men

143

for their upbuilding, their encouragement, their consolation" (I Cor. 14:3).

All this gives us reasons why we should prophesy *in the community*. But what is the gift and how does it operate?

Prophecy is sometimes translated "speaking God's message," and that's what it basically is: to witness what God wants to say to a particular group of people at this particular time. The Old Testament prophets repeat over and over, "Thus says the Lord, your God . . ." to emphasize that the essential quality of prophecy is that it is really God who is speaking. This is the work of the Holy Spirit who "has spoken through the prophets" (Profession of Faith) and who makes the disciples witnesses to Jesus (Acts 1:8).

Prophecy is by no means limited to foretelling the future. Generally, God uses prophecy to communicate what He thinks about His people and what He wants them to do. Most of all, God tells us what He's like in prophecy. St. Thomas Aquinas describes it in terms of a loving relationship:

> Of course this is the proper mark of friendship: that one reveal his secrets to his friend. . . "I will not now call you servants but friends . . ." (John 15:15). Therefore, since by the Holy Spirit we are established as friends of God, fittingly enough it is by the Holy Spirit that men are said to receive the revelation of the divine mysteries.
>
> *(Summa Contra Gentiles,* Bk. 4, Chap. 21:5)

Prophecy is God speaking as a friend to His people. At least this is the predominant way we experience prophecy in our community. Someone listens to God in prayer and tells what he hears to the group. This isn't a revelation of new dogma. It is a message consistent with Scripture and tradition which is spoken in the "convincing power of the Spirit" (I Cor. 2:4) so that people really believe that God loves them and is caring for them. It is often very simple, like "Remember my wounds" or "When you are truly one in mind and heart, then I will give you the work that I want for you." In our group most of the prophecies speak of the intense way God loves us and how He wants us to turn to Him so that He can share that love with us. This is what

God has been telling us over and over: repent, seek Me first by accepting My love for you. This is nothing new, but there is a power in God's own words which is like a two-edged sword which cuts through to where the bone and marrow meet (Hebrews 4:12). This means that the message God speaks is something that we need to hear. It changes as we change to emphasize different aspects of the Gospel. Sometimes the Lord will tell us we're doing a really good job and to relax in Him; at other times it's go out and die to yourself and be witnesses by your love. Prophecy then becomes a continual discernment of God's will for us — what He wants us to repent of and what we should find hope in.

An interesting example of this is the way our community was named the "Children of Joy." Our group has a lot of intellectual skeptics (I'm one of them) who thought this whole idea of community names was too much like college fraternities to be taken seriously. Well, about sixty of us went to the 1971 Notre Dame Charismatic Conference; and when we were praying together, there was a prophecy that we were the Lord's "children of joy." It just so happened that one of the group had already written that on his name tag. We got a little excited about the coincidence, but we really didn't want a name so we waited a little longer to discern what the Lord had in mind. At our next prayer meeting, a seminarian who wasn't at Notre Dame and had not been around for about two months also prophesied that we were the "children of joy." That was even more interesting, but still not convincing. Finally a priest who likewise hadn't been around for months prophesied that we were to be the "children of joy." At last we decided that maybe the Lord wanted to give us a name, no matter how dubious we were about it.

St. Paul says that "...he who prophesies builds up the church" (I Cor. 14:4) and "...speaks to men for their upbuilding, their encouragement, their consolation" (I Cor. 14:3). Real prophecy will effect something in the community. The Christian life is a challenge to grow. Sometimes we lose our perspective, so the Lord refocuses our vision. When things get rough and we start to despair, He consoles us with His word of love. Hearing and responding to prophecy increases our faith and experiential knowledge of God. He "encourages" us to accept the difficult task of loving as He loved and calls us to follow Him to the cross.

A striking instance of this was in September of 1971 when we had lost about half our members during the very trying summer. There were only about thirty-five people at the prayer meeting, and all of us were saddened, wondering whether the group would survive. Well, the Lord spoke: "You have not failed; it's just that you're starting to succeed." The power of the message hit everyone, and all felt a tremendous joy. It wasn't merely that the Lord changed our feeling; but more and more people started coming to the meetings, and in three months we joined together in a covenanted community.

The word of God is powerful and able to transform us. A message of peace, if we respond to it, will bring us peace.

INSPIRATION

A good question at this point is: "If this is for me, how does prophecy work? How is someone inspired?" Most of us would tend to think of prophecy as something mysterious and spectacular — some kind of unique pipeline from God which is denied to ordinary humans like us. This might have been true in Old Testament times when God anointed (or delegated) a few individuals to be His spokesmen. Yet, even then, He promised a new era:

> Then afterward I will pour out
> my spirit upon all mankind.
> Your sons and daughters shall prophesy,
> your old men shall dream dreams,
> your young men shall see visions. . . .

(Joel 3:1)

The days are coming, says the Lord, when I will make a new covenant with the house of Israel . . . No longer will they have need to teach their friends and kinsmen how to know the Lord. All, *from least to greatest,* shall know me. . . .

(Jeremiah 31:31, 34)

In this same vein is the scene in the ancient book of Numbers, where the Lord takes "some of the spirit" that is on Moses and distributes it to the seventy elders. When the elders started prophesying, it shook up some of the people in the camp. Joshua went up to Moses and said, "Moses, my lord, stop them." But Moses replied, "Would that the Lord might bestow his spirit on them all!" (Numbers 11:24-30)

St. Paul, therefore, could say to the Christians of his day, "You can all speak your prophecies, but one by one, so that all may be instructed and encouraged" (I Cor. 14:31). All Christians are baptized in water and the Holy Spirit, and if they are open to the Spirit in faith, any one of them can prophesy. This is part of our share in the life of Jesus, "in the priestly, prophetic, and royal office of Christ" (Vatican II, *Decree on the Apostolate of the Laity*, art. 2).

So, then, the first thing to remember about the charismatic gift of prophecy is that it is not the preserve of a spiritual elite.

The manner in which a person receives a prophetic inspiration is similar to the process of listening to God in prayer. It is "the still small voice" of God within us.

So then, something dissimilar from everyday experience happens when a person receives an inspiration. Usually he notices a sign or indication that God wants him to speak. Some people call this an "anointing," which means a delegation or commissioning by God. The anointing can be practically anything — a physical sensation of God's presence, an imaginative picture of what God wants to say, or just a general sense of urgency or desire to speak for God. I don't know of anyone who has ever physically heard the voice of God.

As to the content of the message, this too is received in many ways. Some people just get a sense that the Lord wants them to speak out the love shown in His passion. So, after praying, they just start speaking about that from a first person point of view. Other people imagine the words or "hear" entire sentences as they pray. Some people see a picture in their minds; and very, very rarely, someone sees a vision.

All of these are in the long run unreliable and uncertain in terms of proving that an inspiration is from God. They are indications that God *might* want you to speak. Generally, the principle that John of the Cross applied to private inspirations applies here as well — the quality or intensity of a sensible consolation, vision or message is *no* sign that is from God. We are never certain. There is always a risk, which includes our faith to witness to Jesus. It is only when we speak a prophecy to the community for their discernment that we can ever know if it is really from God.

The history of Christianity is littered with people who have trusted their own private inspirations more than the discernment of the Church, Scripture and tradition. The results are usually disastrous. Montanus, who received the charism of prophecy in the third century, ended up proclaiming himself the "incarnation of the Holy Spirit." Even more fantastic were two early Quakers, George Nader and Jeremiah Wilson (a woman) who declared themselves to be Jesus Christ in the flesh. The fault isn't with the gift of prophecy or with inspirations; the problem is discernment without the authority of the Church. But because people have tried to exercise the gift of prophecy in the past and made a mess of things is no reason for us to give up and "throw the baby out with the bath water." After all, how many people have sincerely attempted Christianity and made a mess of things? How many saints have led holy but psychologically unbalanced lives? And how often has the enthusiasm of the faithful produced excesses, weird devotions, persecution and even warfare? So we learn from the mistakes of those who, as St. Francis de Sales said, are "to be admired (for their faith) but not to be imitated." And we test all things but hold on to the good (I Thessalonians 5:21) submitting all inspiration to the discernment of the church community.

Knowing these dangers sets us free from taking our own inspirations too seriously. Then we can follow St. Paul's advice: "Set your hearts on spiritual gifts — above all, the gift of prophecy" (I Cor. 14:1). So we tell people to step out in faith and experiment with these gifts. The reason for this is that prophecy can't be discerned by the individual. It is only when it is spoken to the community that there's something to discern. And by speaking the truth in love (Eph. 4:15) we hope to confirm or purify a gift. There are bound to be mistakes which need to be corrected in love so that this gift can improve, comfort and encourage God's people.

RESPONDING TO INSPIRATION

As to how to exercise or yield to the charism of prophecy, we first have to realize that it is not our possession. It is a momentary inspiration which may be experienced only once in an entire lifetime. It is an actual grace which God gives people, not because they are holy but because they are open to receive this gift in faith. "If I have the gift of prophecy ... but have not love, I am nothing" (I Cor. 13:2). The only thing prophesying proves about your life is that you're open to a non-meritorious gift of prophecy. Grasping this fact frees us from the fear of wondering if people will ask, "Who does he think he is?" There is no way you can be proud of prophesying. One time God used a jack-ass to speak His word (Numbers 22:28-30), so you're not boasting when you prophesy. St. Thomas said:

> God's gifts are not always bestowed on those who are simply the best, but sometimes are given to those who are best as regards the receiving of this or that gift. Accordingly, God grants the gift of prophecy to those whom He judges best to give it.
>
> *(Summa Theologica,* II-II, Quest. 172, Art. 5)

I want to share some of my experiences in exercising the gift of prophecy. My community has discerned that I have authentically prophesied in a regular way over the last three years. They also discerned some glaring mistakes. The way I first prophesied was funny. It was my second or third prayer meeting, and there were people present who were using this gift in a way that really touched me. So I prayed, "Lord, help me to do that so that I can comfort them in the same way." Later on, as I was praying in silence, I just felt that the Lord wanted to say, "Come." The more I prayed, the more insistent the still small voice became: "Come!" Now all of these other people were uttering beautiful sentences, and I wasn't going to make a fool out of myself by saying one word. So I asked Him to tell me more; but there it was, even stronger, "Come!" Just then everyone started praying very loud. So I told the Lord, "If you want me to say this, make everyone shut up." Absolute silence ensued. But I was obstinate, and eventually I worked myself up to an emotional pitch of resistance: "I won't, I won't — okay." And I screamed with all the force of my 240 pounds, "COME!!" Everyone jumped three inches off his chair. And I was drained from the emotion I had bottled up. It was generally agreed that if in the future I felt the Lord inspiring me, I should speak sooner — and much, much more quietly.

As I followed the group's instruction, it became easier for me to distinguish inspiration from imagination. What really helped was that our leader and other people would tell me when they felt a prophecy was from God or when it was from me. For instance, one time about two years ago a small group of friends decided to pray for a while. They asked me to join them because "they needed a prophet." Of course I immediately felt I had to prophesy, whether the Lord wanted me to or not. So I made sure to say the first thing which came to mind since I didn't want to disappoint anyone. When I said something which was greeted with a restless silence, I opened my eyes and saw them all shaking their heads. I think I then said, "Well, you can't blame a guy for trying." It took me a couple of weeks till I had the confidence to try again, this time with a better motivation.

I cite these mistakes simply because they can happen to anyone. My community has been able to discern this gift as authentic in spite of a few mistakes which will probably occur again. No one is an oracle, least of all myself. I think this has been the common experience in the Charismatic Renewal. In exercising the gifts, we are once in a while allowed to fail, gracefully. If prophesying is no sign of holiness, then a mistaken prophecy is no sign that you're not with the Lord. Again, we can relax and not take ourselves too seriously.

Recognizing that prophecy is a service to be used in love sets us free to seek this gift for the common good of the community. The first step here, as always, is prayer. Ask God to use you in this way. Ask Him to help you use this gift responsibly. Generally we are open to the gifts of the Spirit when we seek the Giver, not the gifts. The key to prayer and to prophecy is to focus on Jesus and His love for us and then to listen to Him. As Aquinas said, prophecy is an expression of friendship, and it is when we are most friends with God that we listen to Him. It is in the Holy Spirit who is love that "we have the mind of Christ" (I Cor. 2:16) and can speak for Him.

As I said before, there are a variety of ways that people are inspired or accept a message from God. The important thing is to speak out to the group. This means overcoming some fears and inhibitions. It most of all entails a *conscious choice* to use this gift in service. God will not force you or give extraordinary signs that will prove that you're to do this. We need an expectant faith if we are to be open to prophecy.

Probably the easiest way to yield to the gift of prophecy is to seek it in a small group prayer experience. The more you know and trust the people you're praying with, the easier it is to take the risk of exercising the gifts of the Spirit. If you consistently experience being accepted as the person you are, then the fear of being rejected for making mistakes is greatly lessened. Because of this closeness, it is also easier for your friends to help you discern in love an authentic use of the gift of prophecy. Small groups also help us to yield to the charisms because we can't hide in the crowd and expect someone else who's "better at it" to prophesy. If there are only five people together, then the Lord has to use one of us, and "if not me, who?"

It also helps to seek information about how other people yield to the gifts. If you attend certain prayer meetings, ask one of the leaders to help you discern and seek this gift. If there's someone who has a recognized and regular gift of prophecy, talk to him about the practicalities of yielding to this gift. Question the leaders about discerning what goes on in the prayer meeting. If you feel inspired to give a prophecy, *seek discernment* from the leadership after the meeting.

In yielding to an inspiration to prophesy, it is helpful to:
1) Pray for the gift

2) Seek the Giver, not the gift
3) Choose to speak out in faith
4) Seek information and the discernment of authority.

DISCERNING TRUE PROPHECY

How do we discover what authentic prophecy is? Are' there any standards by which I can "test" a prophecy?

First of all this testing or discernment of a gift of the Holy Spirit is something that the Spirit does for us. It just makes sense that if the Spirit wants to speak in prophecy, the same Spirit will give us the means to recognize when that really happens.

> Now instead of the spirit of the world, we have received the Spirit that comes from God to teach us to understand the gifts that He has given us ... An unspiritual person is one who does not accept anything of the Spirit of God: he sees it all as nonsense; it is beyond his understanding because *it can only be understood by means of the Spirit.* A spiritual man is able to judge the value of every-thing ... we are those who have the mind of Christ. (I Cor. 2:12ff)

If we are living in the Holy Spirit, then we will be able to recognize the workings of the Holy Spirit. This is what the Church has called the "sense of faith" of the Christian community. When we are in touch with the Lord, there is a rightness about the things of the Lord: "I know my sheep and my sheep know me" (John 10:14). The Good Shepherd Jesus goes ahead of them "and the sheep follow him because they *recognize his voice*" (John 10:4).

What is important here is that this is a matter of faith and of being in touch with the person of Jesus. It is not magic; it is recognizing the voice of the God who loves and shares His life with you every day. It is basically a community affair, since the family Spirit is recognized by all the children of the family of God.

As the mistakes of history will tell us, there is much more to discernment than this. However, this "sense of faith" is the basic arena for discernment, since Christianity would be a hoax if we did not believe that God wants everyone to know who He is.

Discernment means "to see through something" to the source of the activity. It is not guessing a person's psychological motivation. We "see through" in faith to the origin of the inspiration. A person could be inspired from three sources: the Holy Spirit, his own imagination or good ideas (sincere or insincere), or, very rarely, by evil spirits. (In three years of meetings, I think I heard only one prophecy that might have had an evil inspiration. So I won't talk about this kind of discernment).

Since this seems a bit extraordinary already, I'd like to say that a lot of discernment has to do with that aspect of the "sense of faith" called common sense. If a statement is obviously bizarre, offensive or unloving, it's a matter of Christian common sense to ignore it. For example, that "evil" prophecy I mentioned above was given by a person who was at his first meeting. The man shouted something to the effect that the United States would quickly become Communist (among many other things). This message was so contrary to the love and gentleness of the rest of the meeting that most people didn't need to be told that this wasn't from the Lord.

GUIDELINES

In addition to this common sense, there are other principles which have proven helpful. These are not so much a checklist as general ways in which the Spirit works in the Christian life. It's to be expected that the Spirit will work in prophecy in a manner consistent with all of the other ways Christians experience Him:

1) *Scripture and Tradition:* There is no new revelation since the Apostolic Era. Prophecy does not give us a new Gospel; it makes the age-old message powerful and new. Most prophecy is not only consistent with the teaching of Scripture and tradition, it is often a re-expressing of Scripture in a first person message. The Spirit guides and directs the prophecy to emphasize powerfully aspects of what God had already revealed which are especially needed by this group at this time. Very often,

authentic prophecy will help us to understand the Scripture and tradition of the Church and to apply this to our lives.

2) *Peace and Unity:* This is much of what the general sense of faith of the community is about. Paul says, "God is a God, not of confusion, but of peace" (I Cor. 14:33), and "Make every effort to preserve the unity which has the Spirit as its origin and peace as its binding force" (Ephesians 4:3). Prophecy helps us to have the peace that knows that God is taking care of us. Even if a prophecy challenges us to repent, there is still tranquillity in the group. True prophecy does not divide people into factions but moves people to be more one in mind and heart. Very often this unity is expressed when almost all of the community will recognize a prophecy as authentic and in one voice start thanking and praising God for His word.

3) *Repent! I love you:* In *The Two-edged Sword* John McKenzie says that true Hebrew prophecy was distinguishable from pagan prophecy in that it was always a *personal* message of love which very often disclosed Israel's wrongdoing and demanded repentance as a response. It was not always what the people wanted to hear. Pagan prophecies only glorified the nation's virtue and promised good times. The Lord will often pinpoint our faults, ask us to die to our selfishness and to suffer for Him. This again is nothing extraordinary in terms of the Gospel. As a matter of fact, all prophecy, even the most consoling, should help us to repent and give our lives to the One who loves us, as prayer leads us to resolve to live a more loving life.

4) *"They were cut to the heart"* (Acts 2:37 — RSV): Prophecy will speak to the needs of the group or of certain individuals. This is to me the major proof that prophecy is a way in which God shows His love to His people. Very often someone will have a problem, be depressed or despairing, and a prophecy will say just the right thing to help that person. Therefore a prophecy might not mean much to the majority of the group, but a few will really be touched in a meaningful way.

5) *The spirits of the prophets are under the prophets' control. . ."* (I Cor. 14:32): It is one of the marks of pagan and false prophecy that the prophets need to be in some kind of

ecstasy or trance to prophesy. False prophecy believes that someone has to be possessed by God and lose all control over his faculties in order to prophesy. Hebrew-Christian prophecy is just the opposite. For us, prophecy is something that you consciously choose to do in a way that is peaceful and for the common good. God does not take our free wills away. No prophecy is ever a matter of being *forced* by an anointing, ecstasy or voice so that you are unable to resist. This also means that the one who prophesies is responsible for communicating the message intelligibly and in good order. Whenever someone claims to be under a compulsion to speak, I am skeptical about his inspiration, since Scripture says point blank that he (not any spirit) is in control.

6) *Submission:* The Holy Spirit will work in the leadership and in the whole community to discern a prophecy. It also means that since one of the works of the Spirit is submission to authority, someone who prophesies should be willing to agree with the discernment of the community. No one person has a special pipeline from the Spirit which gives him a truth not shared by the community (including the universal Church). As a matter of practice, when a person claims to have that kind of certain inspiration, it is a sure sign to me that he doesn't have it. There have been many saints who've been inspired by God to preach a certain message to the Church. St. Francis of Assisi, John of the Cross, even Joan of Arc are all examples of people with a prophetic mission who submitted to the discernment of their community even when this discernment seemed contrary to their inspiration. "In any case, judgment as to their [charisms] genuineness and proper use belongs to those who preside over the Church, and to whose special competence it belongs, not indeed to extinguish the Spirit, but to test all things and hold fast to that which is good" (*Dogmatic Constitution on the Church,* art. 12).

7) *"By their fruits you shall know them":* this is the long-term discernment of any Christian action, prophecy or teaching, that it comes from and produces love. If a community responds to authentic prophecy, (among other things) it will grow into a visible love which is the ultimate proof of the

Spirit's presence. This is also true of the individual who regularly uses a gift of the Spirit. Whether it's prophecy, teaching, or healing, the person to trust as being in the Spirit is the one who uses this gift in love. A good example of this is when some people tried to convince St. Teresa of Avila that her inspirations were from the devil. St. Teresa answered to this effect: "Would an evil spirit inspire me to do something which makes me more generous, kind, loving, submissive and peaceful?" The fruit of the Spirit is love, and in the long run this is the only sure sign of His presence.

I have gone into a little detail about these guidelines of discernment simply because they apply not only to prophecy but to all the gifts and to our whole Christian life. If someone is speaking contrary to one of these guidelines, I wouldn't listen to him. In this way the Spirit will protect us if we "test all things and hold fast to that which is good."

TONGUES AND INTERPRETATION

There are many other ways that the Spirit works in prayer meetings besides spontaneous prayer, inspired songs and prophecy. I have used the gift of prophecy as a model of how all the word gifts function and are discerned. So, as I describe the other word gifts, I'll assume that you understand that the way you yield to and use these gifts follows the pattern for prophecy.

> There are different gifts ... One receives the gift of tongues, another that of interpreting the tongues.
>
> (I Cor. 12:4, 10)

> I should like it if all of you spoke in tongues, but I much prefer that you prophesy. The prophet is greater than one who speaks in tongues, unless the speaker can also interpret for the upbuilding of the church.
>
> (I Cor. 14:5)

Paul says that a message in tongues which is interpreted for the benefit of the church is equal to a message in prophecy. He is not referring to the gift of praying in tongues, since he discourages that in public worship: "If the uninitiated or unbelievers should come in when the whole church is assembled and everyone is speaking in tongues, would they not say that you are out of your minds?" (I Cor. 14:23). An inspired message in tongues is one in which one person speaks in tongues to the entire group, and then in prayer the same person or someone else receives an interpretation of that message. The interpretation is not a translation by someone who knows the language being spoken, but rather an inspiration of the Holy Spirit.

Occasionally people of questionable psychological stability have spoken out in tongues in the middle of sermons or liturgies. Part of the reason for this is that it's a very easy thing to speak out in tongues. I mean it comes naturally to Pentecostals, when they are feeling excited in prayer, to want to speak in tongues. As understandable as this is, it most probably is not inspiration. An inspiration in tongues is received the same way a prophecy is. We are just as likely to be mistaken about tongues as about prophecy or anything else, and just because there has been an interpretation is no sure sign that either the tongues or the interpretation is from the Holy Spirit.

In our community we experience this gift rather less frequently than a simple prophetic message. When the Spirit works this way, it really is a sign for the uninitiated, as Paul says. Once at one of our open meetings, I was inspired to sing in tongues and then sing the interpretation-message. Naturally I was a little worried as to how the new people would take it. One man, a psychologist who was there for the first time, came up to me and said that while he could rationally explain away tongues as a release of the unconscious, the message I had given was "too beautiful" to be anything but God.

Of course, it's really handy to have someone around who has a learned knowledge of the language used in this gift. This has happened a few times, most impressively when our leader, Fr. Lange, was addressing a conference in Lafayette, Louisiana. At the prayer meeting a woman spoke in tongues and interpreted; everyone was strengthened in faith by this message. Another woman did the same, but the group felt uneasy about her message. Later on, Fr. Lange was conversing with a Scripture scholar who happened to understand the languages spoken (different dialects of Syrian). The first message was a perfect translation; the second, which had been discerned as questionable, was not even a remote translation. As consoling as this type of confirmation is, it happens extremely rarely. The main point to remember is that using this gift responsibly can really increase the faith of the community.

WITNESSING

> To one the Spirit gives wisdom in discourse, to another the power to express knowledge.
>
> (I Cor. 12:8)

Generally these are gifts of witnessing and teaching in the power of the Spirit. Witnessing (or testifying) is simply narrating or describing some way in which Jesus has been working in your life. This is what all Christians are supposed to be doing in their everyday life and conversation. In community meetings it is a witness which is inspired for the whole group. The witness can be about big things or little things. It can be the story of a conversion, a healing, a new insight or painful perseverance — the content doesn't matter that much. What does matter is that the witness is inspired for the purpose of bolstering the faith of the whole group. Just recently I gave a witness about a rather long period of dryness and aridity in my personal prayer life and how the Lord taught me to seek Him for Himself, not for His gifts. The lesson of the story was my noticing a Cracker Jack box bearing the motto: "The more you eat, the more you want." Silly as it sounds, this slogan described to me the process of loving and being drawn to Jesus through these dry spells. The more you have of Jesus, the more you want Him. Well, this was apparently what a lot of people in the community were going through, and the Spirit helped us to have faith and seek the Lord even in the darkness.

Witnessing is sharing what Jesus is doing in your life and the life of others. It is a basic way we build up one another's faith. The thing that really matters about witnessing at prayer meetings is not so much how spectacular the event was, but that the witness be inspired by the Spirit and given in love.

Witnessing satisfies our desire to see that God is really working among His people. In addition to that, we all have the need to grow in our *understanding* and practice of our faith and love. The Spirit responds to these needs by giving us the teaching gifts, or as Paul says, "wisdom in discourse" and "the power to express knowledge." These gifts *can* be manifested in sermons, Christian instruction, books, prayer meetings, etc. — any time a person teaches in the power of the Holy Spirit.

THE WORD OF WISDOM

We understand "wisdom in discourse" to be an inspired insight into the way we live our Christian lives. It is very often a solution to a difficult problem or a sense of what Jesus asks of us in a particular situation. This does not necessarily mean that the person uttering the wisdom is habitually wise; rather, he received a momentary inspiration given in a particular situation. This can happen in counseling sessions, in daily life or in formal teaching, but I want to limit my examples to prayer meetings.

A little over two years ago, our group was together praying and trying to decide whether the Lord wanted us to make a covenant with Him and each other. There was disagreement and conflict until a young woman, who had never before shared at a meeting, stood up. She said that the way we had been living together was just like a man and woman living together. Maybe the Lord wanted us to take this risk and be married to Him. That settled things for most people. And even though I was against the whole idea, I knew that what she had said was true and from the Spirit. You see, you don't have to accept an inspired message. I was hostile to this one for about two more months.

The word of wisdom can also be something very simple to help us practice our faith. Just recently another young woman spoke out at our open prayer meeting for the first time. She said that Christian life was intensely simple. She had been thinking about love and breath. To breathe, you have to inhale and exhale. If you only inhale, you choke. For a Christian to live, he has to accept or inhale the love of God and then give that love to his neighbor. If he holds it in, he chokes: so love is like breath.

We've also seen this gift work to solve personal problems. As obvious as the above message was, it touched me in a powerful way and helped me relate to a certain person I had been trying to love.

THE WORD OF KNOWLEDGE

The gift of knowledge or instruction also meets definite present needs that people have. We often experience this in the context of formal teaching. It normally involves presenting the truth of Christian doctrine in such a way that it is really understandable to people and helps them to give their lives to God. Arnold Bittlinger describes it as "... the old message spoken in the new situation in such a way that it still remains the old message" (*Gifts and Graces,* p. 30. This is, in my opinion, the best book available on the charismatic gifts.) You might say that this power of the Spirit to speak the old message in a new way solves our problems of "being relevant."

This is nothing new in the Church. People were awed at hearing Francis of Assisi speak of the love of God. People journeyed hundreds of miles to experience the love and wisdom of the Cure of Ars in the confessional. Many times in the lives of the saints you read of people being converted through a chance sentence or a phrase in a sermon.

There are many ways that we have experienced this gift in our prayer meetings. Someone might explain a passage of Scripture so that it gives meaning to our present situation. More frequently it has been a message which explains a basic truth of the Christian life in a way that makes it alive and fresh. Often the message does not come from clergymen or teachers but from those who (as Aquinas said) were best suited to exercise that gift. One young man in our community is particularly open to this gift of knowledge. Though he is very intelligent, he is, through no fault of his own, not the most articulate person in the world. Yet the teachings he gives have such power that they literally astound the community. One night he got up and spontaneously gave a beautiful discourse on the theme:

"Freedom means that we are free to discover God in everything we do." After he sat down, one of the older men, an executive, said, "No insult to our brother, but I know that he wasn't capable of that kind of thinking by himself. It had to be the Lord. This is why I come here, because the Lord speaks through you people."

Again, what's important is that the Lord inspires the message. At any meeting there may be several people with the theological background to speak on any random topic. But orthodox doctrine is no sure indication that a speech is a Spirit-given word gift. The determining factor is that we witness, teach, prophesy what *God* wants said. Everything at a prayer meeting should be inspired in this way. Whether it's singing a song, reading Scripture, a poem, exhorting people to praise and worship – all of it should be the movement of the Spirit. Any Christian can be open to use these word gifts in faith to build up the community. As regards seeking and discerning these gifts, the same guidelines apply here as to prophecy.

ATTITUDES

> So my dear brothers, what conclusion is to be drawn? At all your meetings, let *everyone be ready* with a psalm or a sermon or a revelation, or ready to use his gift of tongues or to give an interpretation; but *it must always be for the common good.*
>
> (I Cor. 14:26 – JB)

What then should be our attitude toward prayer meetings? First of all, a basic *expectant faith* which says that Jesus is present through His Spirit and will lead us, inspire us and speak to us. We come to celebrate and to enjoy this loving, transforming presence of God. This necessitates prayer that we will be open to the impulses of the Spirit. The quality of each individual relationship with Jesus will affect the quality of the community prayer and worship. As we become a community which is one in mind and heart, the Lord can more clearly speak to us and guide us. Tnis means that even in the prayer meeting every act of praise and exercise of a charism is an expression of love and service for my brothers and sisters. The love we share, then, is the arena or vehicle of the action of the Holy Spirit of Love.

Much of what happens at a prayer meeting is our *receiving from God* in faith. We respond to what Jesus is saying to the community in the same way we give ourselves: in an attitude of expectant faith, prayer, love, and service. The word of God is also heard. in the power of the Spirit. While we "Test everything" we "Do not stifle the Spirit" or "... despise prophecies" (I Thess. 5:19-21). Just think of how wonderful it is that God talks to us in Scripture and in the word gifts. We should never let anyone's personality or our own prejudices get in the way of listening to Jesus speaking to us through our brothers.

This demands humility. We have to be both humble and honest to exercise and hear the word gifts of the Spirit. As Paul writes the Corinthians who thought they were special because of these gifts:

> Not many of you are wise, as men account wisdom; not many are influential; and surely not many are wellborn. God chose those whom the world considers absurd to shame the wise; he singled out the weak of this world to shame the strong. He chose the world's lowborn and despised, those who count for nothing, to reduce to nothing those who were something; so that mankind can do no boasting before God ... This is just as you find it written, "Let him who would boast, boast in the Lord."
>
> (I Cor. 1:26-31)

To put all this in a larger perspective: we must always keep in mind that charismatic prayer is only one of the treasures of church worship. In terms of calling people to a loving relationship with Jesus and the Father through the experienced power of the Spirit, you could say that it is basic to all Christians. In this way it represents the experienced faith-renewal of the Sacraments of Baptism and Confirmation. But as a style or form of prayer, it is only one mode of worship among many. As far as speaking and hearing God's word, it is but one of many. It demands an integration into the broader life of church worship and church teaching. For the Catholic (charismatic or otherwise), the center of this life will always be the eucharistic community and the word of God in Scripture and tradition. This is merely to say that our life is to be Christ-centered, not charism-centered.

And so we shall all come together to that oneness in our faith and in our knowledge of the Son of God; we shall become mature men, reaching to the very height of Christ's full stature. Then we hall no longer be children, carried by the waves, and blown about by every shifting wind of the teaching of deceitful men, who lead others to error by the tricks they invent. Instead, by speaking the truth in a spirit of love, we must grow up in every way to Christ, who is the head. Under his control all the different parts of the body fit together, and the whole body is held together by every joint with which it is provided. So when each separate part works as it should, the whole body grows and builds itself up through love.

(Ephesians 4:13-16)

BIBLIOGRAPHY

RECOMMENDED READING:

Bittlinger, Arnold, *Gifts and Graces: A Commentary on I Corinthians 12-14,* William B. Eerdmans Publishing Co., Grand Rapids, Michigan, 1967, 126pp.
A rather complete study of the nature and function of the charismatic gifts. Most balanced, theologically sound and experience-oriented book you can find on the subject.

Clark, Stephen, *Spiritual Gifts*, Dove Publications, Pecos, New Mexico, 1969, 35pp.
  A clear, practical explanation of the experience and function of the charismatic gifts.

Gee, Donald, *Concerning Spiritual Gifts*, Gospel Publishing House, Springfield, Missouri, 1972, 119pp.
  Basic teaching on the gifts—their use and abuse—from a classical Pentecostal viewpoint.

SUPPLEMENTARY READING:

Cavnar, Jim, *Prayer Meetings*, Dove Publications, Pecos, New Mexico, 1969, 35pp.
  The practical "hows and whys" of charismatic prayer.

by Joseph Lange

Growing into a Deeper
Relationship with God ⑨

Living with God — with Jesus and the Father and the Spirit — is a sharing of our lives with someone. Each step in the concrete living reality of that shared life is a matter of conscious choice. To begin with, then, we are talking about five things, and each of them is important. I'd like to repeat that: *each of them is important.* The five things are (1) Growth procceds by steps; (2) It involves and is a concrete living reality; (3) We are talking about sharing our lives; (4) It requires that we be aware or conscious of what we are doing; and (5) It involves decisions.

FREELY CHOOSING

Let's begin with the last item mentioned: growing into a shared life with the Lord involves a choice. Each step of the way requires that we choose something. The Lord made us free, and He always respects that freedom. Our freedom comes into play by our selecting those things which will help us to grow in our relationship with Him. In one sense, each step is a decision; or, conversely, each decision is a step. We go as far and as deep as we determine. We go when we choose and as we choose.

This is *not* to imply that the gift of God's love for us or the deepening of the relationship with Him is created by our choice; rather, it is only to say that God's love for us initially and continually can touch us and work in us only to the extent that we decide to allow that to happen. I'll never be touched by

165

another's love for me if I cannot believe that it is true and real and sincere. I'll never really be changed by another's love for me if I do not decide to trust in the sincerity of that person. If I do choose to trust, then my life will never be the same, for I have allowed the power of another's love to reach me. I am now bound by ties of loyalty and mutual trust, of patience and generosity, not as something extrinsic, but from deep within the heart.

Before I can make that choice (or that series of choices, one by one), before I risk my life and stake my future on the fidelity and sincerity of another, I simply must know something about the other person as well as the consequences of choosing to believe in him. To think that one can authentically love without such knowledge is to be caught up in romanticism. Each of us plays games with this, but deep down we know they are games; and we are talking here of going deep down, of getting past the games.

One could write a great deal about the obstacles to loving and the games we play, but let us cut through all that and get to what we need to know, to that fundamental confrontation with the person of Jesus and His Father and the Spirit. What I am trying to say is that it is not enough that our relationship with the Lord be only implicit. It is not enough to say, "Lord, I wish to share my whole life with you." In the beginning, perhaps, that's about as clear and precise as we can get — or need to get. But growth comes only to the extent that we get down to specifics, and that occurs only as we begin to make explicit all the implications of such a choice. That happens as we look at our experience and the concrete reality of our lives. We have to look at how we spend our free time, how we spend our money, the kinds of commitments we have, our thoughts, our feelings, our desires. Only as we make the effort to reflect on these things, to bring them explicitly to awareness, only then can we consciously choose to surrender them to the Lordship of Jesus, only then can we consciously choose to share these aspects of our lives with Him. This is to say, that experiences are essential for growth; for it is only in such reflection that it becomes clear what we have truly given to the Lord and what we have as yet left untouched and unredeemed. One reason for teaching in general and for these teachings in particular is to bring to awareness and to make more explicit those areas of our lives about which we have to choose if we are to grow in the Lord.

SHARING ALL THINGS WITH JESUS

I've said that growth in the Lord means a "sharing of our lives with Him." Through courtship and years of marriage, couples who grow into a deep loving relationship find a number of things happening to them. They begin to experience each other in a variety of everyday moods and fears and desires and actions. Paradoxically, as their individual lives become gradually fused into a common life, their individualities and unique characteristics become enhanced. I find myself as I lose myself. I become more of me as I share my life with another. A new husband's response to invitations gradually shifts from "I" to "we." More and more there is the "Wait till I check with my wife," and from "I'd like to do that" to "We'd like to do that." In our relationship with Jesus and the Father, there develops a "Wait till I check with the Lord" response to invitations — one of the ways in which we pray.

But, sharing our lives with the Lord involves more than spending time alone with Him in prayer. I'm sure that as you meditate on what it is to share your life with Jesus, He will teach you many things. It means, among other things, sharing your thoughts and your speech, your comings and goings, your free time and your work, your recreation and your rest, your affections, your attachments, your commitments — all things large and small. "Whatever you do, whether in speech or in action, do it in the name of the Lord Jesus. Give thanks to God the Father through Him" (Col. 3:17).

What we have been talking about is living with Jesus, sharing our lives with Him by conscious, deliberate choice. It is this which makes living "with Christ" a concrete reality, a reality which begins when we first repent of our rebelliousness and self-sufficiency and surrender our lives to His Lordship. Then, day by day and week by week, we gradually learn to fuse our

167

lives with Him. We get to know Him better. We learn to trust Him more. We grow in appreciation of His infinite love and forbearance and patience and mercy. We confide in Him. We begin to experience that growing in Him means growing into His body, means living in a community of those who also follow the Lord. It means coming to appreciate the concrete living reality of how God's love for us makes all things new. Our conversations become new, our habits become new, our relationships with others become new, our emotional life and our thoughts become new; each aspect of our everyday life becomes new in its freedom and peace and joy as we become together one in mind and heart in the unity of His Spirit.

GROWTH

Finally, to wrap up this section, as we grow we realize that growth proceeds by steps. Occasionally there is a quantum leap, a clear change in direction, but most often there is just a gradual change which can only be noticed after a period of time has elapsed. As we continue, we must never lose sight of the struggles that it takes to grow; the struggle to face ourselves honestly; the struggle to achieve clarity; the struggle to surrender; the struggle to accept love in trust; the struggle to maintain hope; the struggle to put up with others; the struggle to accept our weakness. One could go on indefinitely. It is an aspect of our experience which needs to be reflected on at least until we have achieved a tranquility about our own failings and the failings of others. As long as we have not come to terms with growth ourselves, as long as we have not yet appreciated deeply and deeply accepted our own weakness, we shall always expect more from ourselves and from others than we have any reasonable hope of experiencing. This leads to frustration, resentment, anger, and depression, a breaking off of communication, a breakdown of the unity of the Body.

Also, we grow in stages. There will always be members of the community who are at early, middle, and mature stages of growth. A unity of mind and heart among them would be impossible if it were not for the healing, forgiving, accepting love of God for us, which makes it possible for us to accept ourselves and others. We need to reflect on this, we need to accept it.

Further, not only do we grow by stages, we grow at different rates. In a family, the husband may grow more quickly than the wife, or vice-versa. Members of the community grow at different rates. Each one of us has been affected by innumerable unique experiences, a history which makes our healing and transformation an extremely complicated and delicate matter. The right time and remedy varies for each of us. How can there be uniform growth and uniform response? Fortunately, it is not our problem. The Lord knows the complexity of it all; and He, with His infinite wisdom and His personal caring, will transform each of us as He knows is best. For us, it is important to realize only that it is wise to leave all of this in His hands and relax. One of the ways in which our loving Jesus brings us peace is in the knowledge and trust that the transforming of each soul is His work, not ours — except to the extent that He shows us how He wants us to collaborate. The rest we peacefully leave to Him, knowing that, not only is He the only one who can transform each of us, but also that He wants to.

Growth in our relationship with the Father, Jesus and the Spirit also requires some attention to other factors. We'll take them one at a time.

1. *Our life together.* We are devoting several chapters to this; it is so important. Here it is sufficient to highlight the dimensions of growth. Read I Corinthians 12-14 again, where Paul speaks both about the power and gifts of the Spirit and of our being together the Body of Christ. Re-read Ephesians 4. Pray about it. Meditate on it.

Paul expects each of us to appreciate our call to follow Jesus together, to be aware of the gift He has given each of us for the building up of the Body. He expects us to love the Body of Jesus as intensely as we love the risen Lord Himself. He expects us to appreciate the organic relationship which now exists between ourselves and all the other members of the Body. We are members of one Body, the Body of Christ. We are called to grow *together* into the fullness of the Messianic Presence. We are totally dependent on each other. If you suffer, I suffer. If you are in sin, I am poorer.

If our life together is rich in the works of the Spirit because each one is contributing his or her gift and we are all earnestly praying that God will bless our life together with an abundance of gifts, then I am surrounded by God's presence and power. My faith is sustained. I am encouraged and consoled. I am constantly encountering the reality of God's Kingdom. On the other hand, if each of us is not praying that God will bless us with an abundance of gifts, then I will not be sustained by the constant manifestations of the Spirit. Something which God wants to provide for me will be missing. I will be undernourished, sickly, and weak. Your fidelity to all this affects me this way. My fidelity affects you. We are members of one another. If I am to be made well and if I am to grow into the fullness of the Spirit, then each of you has a part in it simply by yielding to the Spirit yourself and praying for an abundance of gifts in our life together. This comes about through concrete choices and specific actions.

2. *God wants us to be transformed by His love.* He really does. He cares about us, about each of us, and He cares that we become one. We must take time in our personal prayer and in our reading of Scripture, counting on the power of His Spirit to teach us, to come to know and appreciate how much He really cares, how much He really loves each of us. We can also see the effects of His love, His healing, forgiving, transforming love, in the lives of the saints and the lives of members of the community and in the community life itself. As we grow in trust of His love, we will also grow in the confidence of our prayers to be transformed by it, for we will come to deeply appreciate that He really does want us to be saints.

3. *Desire for a closer relationship with God.* Once again, we must consciously choose to desire to share our lives with God. There are many reasons why we may not really want to do that, but they will be the topic of another chapter. At this point, we just want to emphasize that hungering and thirsting for a deeper relationship with God is something we have to choose. Jesus is

committed to us. We might well ask how committed we are to Him, how much we really want Him. "As much as you want me, that is how much I can come to you."

4. *Guidance.* Jesus wants to come to us, and He wants to give us His Spirit, and He wants us to grow. He knows that most of the time we don't know what to do, that we need help and guidance. And, as we come to appreciate the quality of His love for us and His infinite power, we begin to trust more and more in the fact that He will guide us — for He is the Good Shepherd, and we have a Father who is divine and a Comforter who is divine. The Lord Himself will guide us if we are open to His influence around us. Through inspiration, through His word, through the teaching of the Church, and through the circumstances of our lives He guides us and teaches us. It takes discernment to know what is of His Spirit and what isn't in these things, and only the gift of discernment and growth in our relationship with Him help us to see clearly what His will is. As we come more and more to know His mind and His heart through sharing our lives with Him, we find that discernment comes more easily. What is especially important in the beginning and always important in large things is that being "passage happy" is not the best way of seeking the Lord's will and that not every event, feeling and thought is from the Spirit of God. Especially in the beginning, we ought to be aware of the danger and reality of being wrong. We ought to ask help in discernment. That help is provided for in the community, and in the person of a spiritual director. We must continually ask the Lord for discernment and for helpers in the community. This cannot be overemphasized. The Lord really will provide us with help and guidance. Once more, we have to choose to avail ourselves of it.

5. *Small things.* Also, the Lord has told us that if we are faithful about small things, we will be given larger things to do. Fidelity to the Lordship of Jesus simply must concern itself with the mundane little things which make up the fabric of everyday life. Having once turned over our lives to Him, having repented of and turned from the major obstacles to His love, it

171

is time to give the rest. He will show us what He wants us to work on and how He wants us to work on it. We must trust Him to make us new, but we have to choose to admit Him into every aspect of our lives.

6. *Balance.* We ought to begin here by being realistic. There is a mythology about balance, a kind of rationalism which distorts the reality of everyday life. Life is creative, and novelty is forever leaking in. Situations change and we change. The response to certain situations at certain times requires an unusual demand on time, effort, or enthusiasm. If we are to speak of balance, it ought to be in the context of what is an appropriate response to a particular situation, which itself is in the larger context of a more general situation. For example, it's altogether appropriate to be enthusiastic and much absorbed in things spiritual at the beginning of one's new life in Christ, even to the neglect of other things. Enthusiasm and absorption, if properly guided, contribute to a firm and deep foundation. But such behavior might be inappropriate at another stage of one's growth. What I am trying to say is that the balance we must try to achieve is the center about which we oscillate, rather than some fixed distribution of activities, emotions, etc.

On the other hand, growing in the Christian life requires a kind of dynamic overall balance between attention to one's personal relationship with the Lord and reaching out to others, between prayer and action. It requires a similar balance between so-called "spiritual exercises" and the work of the world. We are going to devote chapters to both prayer and action; the point here is that solid growth requires both. In yielding to the Lordship of Jesus, we open our hearts to Him and become part of His Body to be His redeeming presence in the world. It is a distortion to believe that we can be for Jesus just by cultivating our interior life. Rather, we become filled with the Spirit so that Christ's Body may be built up.

The Spirit of God is given us so that *all things* might be made new. Forgetting this point leads to the distortion that language about the spiritual life sometimes creates. In fact, since the sending of the Spirit, there are no longer "spiritual exercises" as opposed to "worldly" ones. Everything is to be done in the Spirit, including work, study, driving the car, taking care of the children. Each thing done in the Spirit is a part, however small, of reclaiming the world for Christ. The fullness of Christian life is found in extending it to the full dimensions of ordinary life. Still, there is a balance to be achieved between prayer and works or between those ways in which we directly work at building a relationship with God and those in which it is less direct. This is similar to the building of a relationship in marriage. Everything contributes to the shared life, but some things (such as sitting down alone together to share) are more directly related to the personal relationship than others (such as going to work or doing the laundry).

Finally, there must develop a balance between life in the community and outreach beyond the community. Unless we take time to be with each other and live with each other in Christ, we will not be a community in fact. On the other hand, if our whole life is spent only in the context of the community, then we can hardly help but become distorted. We'll lose touch with the problems of others and with the problems of reaching out to others. We would become a kind of "hot house" Christian, extremely fragile, as well as insensitive.

God has given Himself to us, Father, Son and Spirit, so that we might grow into a likeness of Himself. Praise Him! He is with us.

BIBLIOGRAPHY

RECOMMENDED READING:

Saint Francis de Sales, *Introduction to the Devout Life,* Image Books, Garden City, New York, 1950, 315pp.

St. Francis integrates intellectual and secular life with the call to reflection in what is now recognized as one of the greatest devotional guides of all time.

Schlink, Basilea, *Repentance—The Joy-filled Life*, Zondervan, Grand Rapids, Michigan, 1966, 61pp. (see chapter 4).
   Daily repentance is the basis of all Christian growth and joy.

SUPPLEMENTARY READING:

Haughton, Rosemary, *The Transformation of Man*, Paulist Press, New York, New York, 1967, 280pp.

by Tony Cushing

The Second Coming:
The Pilgrim Church

10

> My Lord will come again,
> My Lord will come again,
> So sing, my soul, and laugh and shout
>   and skip and run,
> I know my Lord will come.

If the mention of Christ's return creates in you the kind of joy expressed in the song above, then you don't need to read any further. It's a matter of common experience, however, that few people sing at the thought of the Second Coming. Yet we profess at every Eucharist that "we wait in joyful hope for the coming of our Savior, Jesus Christ."

In our general theological perspective, we described the Church as being the tension of the already and the not yet. We are liberated, healed and transformed in an ever growing degree — already changed but not yet totally so. We are the people of God on pilgrimage to a future and abiding city. We have a definite destination which we already behold in Jesus, a fulfillment which is pledged to us by the Spirit who "is the guarantee that we shall receive what God has promised his people, and assures us that God will give complete freedom to those who are his" (Ephesians 1:14 — TEV). We are going somewhere. But what is it going to be like when we get there?

Now, any sensible person who is about to go on an extended

175

journey will have already answered a number of questions. He will have found out what this new city is like. Has anyone I know been there before? Did he like it? Is it worth the expense? How long does it take to get there? Is the journey itself worthwhile and enjoyable? What should I take with me? Are pets allowed? Many Christians, being sensible people, have tried to answer these questions. A lot of the answers have been unsatisfactory, and quite a few of them seem contradictory. What should we do then? Here we are, like a group of vacationers being assaulted by competing travel agencies: "Go here, it's sunny!" "No, go to our place, it's serene!" "Fly, you'll get there in half the time!" "But the boat is a real pleasure." Consequently, faced with all these pressures, most of us remain at home, try to relax, get bored and frustrated, longing for something to happen to get us out of this mess. So we wait with little joy or hope, wondering what's coming next.

For many of us the picture of the Second Coming presented to us in our childhood was probably disagreeable. I can remember being told in elementary school that God knows everything about us and that at the last judgment He's going to show everyone else all the ugly things we thought and did. Immediately I imagined my life being shown at this huge drive-in theater with everyone else giggling at my hard-kept secrets. I was in despair — after all, what's adolescence without the wonders of concealment? There were some alternatives: (1) I could immediately reform my life, thereby dressing up the picture of myself, (2) I could throw morals to the winds and give all those goody-goodies a really exciting movie, (3) I could do my best to ignore this cosmic voyeurism, try to refuse publication and simply accept my fate with dignity. Admittedly I was interested in what other people's secret lives were like, but I assumed that they were as good and as boring as they seemed to be. Why go through all of that embarrassment for an infinity of Heidis? So, somewhat angry at this bossy God, I opted for ignorance and remained smugly terrified of the end of the world. This is somewhat like building a home on a railroad track and trying to convince yourself that a train won't come. At best it's a trifle anxious. If you focus on it enough, it'll make you psychotic.

Mark Twain made a much more reasonable rejection of a childish concept of this future city in his last book, *Letters from Earth*. The gist of the story is something like this: "Can you imagine these dreary prudes and do-gooders all crowded together, dressed in white shrouds, floating on clouds — singing? All the time singing? Why, they couldn't even carry a tune down here, much less play those silly harps. If you can't take an hour of it on Sunday, how in heaven's name will you endure an eternity of it? Not for me; give me a place with some life."

Both Twain and I scorned distorted versions of life in eternity, not the real thing. To find out what the reality is, we need to examine how Jesus described His return and try to extract from His own words what the future glory means to us now, during the pilgrimage.

THE PARABLES OF THE END TIME

The overwhelming impact of the parables of the Second Coming is the *certainty* of Jesus' coming again:

> The Son of Man will come with his Father's glory accompanied by his angels.
>
> I assure you, among those standing here there are some who will not experience death before they see the Son of Man come in his kingship.
>
> (Matthew 16:27, 28)

> So *will* it be at the coming of the Son of Man.
>
> (Matthew 24:39)

> ... the Son of Man will be ashamed of him when he comes with the holy angels in his Father's glory.
>
> (Mark 8:38)

> Then men will see the Son of Man coming in the clouds with great power and glory.
>
> (Mark 13:26)

In the New Testament, the title "Son of Man" is used almost exclusively by Jesus in reference to Himself. It was a title of great significance for the Jews. The Son of Man in the book of Daniel was God's chosen one who would initiate the Kingdom of God. The establishment of this Kingdom was to be the dramatic and final act of God to restore the world in righteousness. Jesus declares this publicly in response to Caiaphas' command: "... tell us if you are the Messiah, the Son of God." Jesus answered: "So you say. But I tell *all* of you: from this time on you will see the Son of Man sitting at the right side of the Almighty and coming on the clouds of heaven!" (Matthew 26:63, 64 — TEV)

And in the parable of the widow and the judge, Jesus refers to His coming in a kind of melancholy, off-hand reference which is to me the most personal and absolute statement of His return: "But when the Son of Man comes, will he find any faith on the earth?" (Luke 18:8) Jesus seems nonchalantly sure of His coming; what is doubtful (as always) is man's response to Him.

IN GLORY

This Second Coming will be different from the first: Jesus will come in power and glory. During His life, Jesus was like one among us whom we do not recognize (John 1:26). People who wonder why Jesus didn't appear with legions of angels need only wait for that "day the Son of Man is revealed" (Luke 17:30). There will no longer be any uncertainty about God — everyone will know that Jesus is the Lord: "As the lightning from the east flashes to the west, so will the coming of the Son of Man be" (Matthew 24:27). This conclusive revelation of Jesus will be the consummation of God's saving plan. He will gather His people to Himself. "When he does, He will repay each man according to his conduct" (Matthew 16:27).

> I come to gather nations of every language; they
> shall come and see my glory . . .
> All mankind shall come to worship
> before me, says the Lord.
>
> (Isaiah 66:18, 23)

> After that will come the end, when, after having
> destroyed every sovereignty, authority and power, he will

hand over the kingdom to God the Father ... When, finally, all has been subjected to the Son, he will then subject himself to the One who made all things subject to him, so that God may be all in all.

(I Cor. 15:24, 28)

A NEW CREATION

It is the Father's plan "... to bring all things in the heavens and on earth into one under Christ's headship (Ephesians 1:10). The love of God will be totally revealed and Jesus will penetrate all of creation — transforming it through and through. Christ will be all and in all. This is the "fullness" or perfection of the Body of Christ. The Greek word *pleroma* that Paul used in Ephesians is simply another term for the Second Coming. It is the harvesting of the universe. The Church is now holy and pure — the spotless bride waiting to be married to the beloved.

"See, I make all things new!" Then he said, ... "These words are already fulfilled! I am the Alpha and the Omega, the Beginning and the End. To anyone who thirsts I will give to drink without cost from the spring of lifegiving water. He who wins the victory shall inherit these gifts; I will be his God and he shall be my son.

(Revelation 21:5-7)

Everything that was revealed and promised by God is brought to pass. We are, in reality, God's children; the new covenant is completely actualized because now God's home is with men (Rev. 21:3).

Perhaps all of this seems too optimistically beautiful. A typical reaction might be: "Yes, that's nice, but what about the moon turning to blood, the stars falling from the sky, and all the guts and gore when the saints go marching in? Isn't that a part of it, too?" I must admit that it's a valid question. And it will take a while to answer it. Most people seem to picture the Second Coming in terms of destructiveness. Now it is true that almost all the apocalyptic language is in terms of warfare and annihilation, but this fact has been overemphasized. The result is that the Second Coming induces terror instead of comfort. For

179

example, it's true that our thoughts and deeds will be revealed in the end. The little story I told in the beginning showed that I concretely grasped that aspect. Yet what I left out was that I would be totally loved as well as totally known. And, of course, to be known without love is terrifying.

Okay, then, how does God pull off a loving destruction of the world? Well, first of all, it's not primarily a destruction but a transformation, "new heavens and a new earth." All of the tribulations and horrors are merely a prelude to something else — "it will be like the pains that come upon a woman who is about to give birth" (1 Thess. 5:3 — TEV). Inevitably there is a degree of dying and pain in every change ". . . but when the child is born she forgets her suffering, because she is happy that a baby has been born into the world" (John 16:21 — TEV). For a lot of people, watching a childbirth is at least unpleasant. But it depends on whether you focus on the pain or on the new creation.

This was really brought home to me a few years ago when a girlfriend and I were teaching a third grade religion class on repentance and confession. All through the class we tried to emphasize the love of the Father, His gentleness, His healing and peace. We had just about gotten it across when one of the kids blurted out in a very excited way, "A man came to our house and told us that God was going to destroy the world and burn everything and everybody in a great big fire." At this news, all the children were terrified and in no mood to confess to some pryomaniac God. We didn't know what to say, so we just sat and prayed. Then we had the right words: "The end of the world is a little like repentance — God is going to put our broken world back together. It's just like if you tried to fix your bike all by yourself, and you got it all goofed up. Your father had to take it apart again in order to fix it. Well, we tried to fix the world ourselves, so in the end, God has to take it apart a little only to fix it. Except that He'll make it perfect — better than new."

Wow, what results! They loved it and asked more about what was going to happen. So we told them, "No more tears or death or pain." They left smiling and saying, "Boy, I can't wait till Jesus comes — it'll be beautiful." In truth this will be the repentance and transformation of the entire universe. "The seed must fall into the ground and die." Most people know that there's a great deal of pain and dying to selfishness involved in trying to love someone. Some things have to go. In the same way, if God is to be totally married to His people, then a few things have to go. Anyone truly in love has to be able to say, "The former things have passed away."

VICTORY OVER EVIL

What disappears at the end is evil, in all forms. This is the third major aspect of the Second Coming: God will be vindicated and evil will be definitively overthrown. If you think this is a little too much like an old-time western, where the guys in the white hats kill the guys in the black hats and get the pretty girls, don't be alarmed — it's close to the truth. The good guys do win. And as anyone who is devoted to western movies knows, there *never* was any doubt that they would win, no matter how sticky the plot became. Every one of us has a suspicion that this is true in life. We all feel that sometime, we don't know when, the good will get what they really deserve and the wicked will be punished. Peter Berger, in his *Rumor of Angels,* says that this is one of the consistent "signs" of God's existence. How can we ever balance the scales for an Adolph Eichmann? Somewhere he has to get what he deserves; therefore God's triumph in the Second Coming.

It's interesting that most of the destructiveness indicated in apocalyptic writings has to do with the destruction of evil (whore of Babylon, the great beast, punishment of evil-doers by fire, etc.).

This isn't too pleasant, but we have to recognize the brute fact that evil exists in a very dramatic way and that someone is responsible for it. That someone is not some Great Impersonal Evil Abstraction, materiality, or even a very personal Satan, but human beings who have rejected Love in all forms. Who they are, we can't tell. Their punishment is to live eternity in the same way they lived on this earth — without God or love or kindness. "The measure with which you measure will be used to measure you" (Matthew 7:2).

This resolution of the problem of evil teaches two important things: 1) though evil surely exists (common sense), it is temporary and merely a distortion of good; 2) God's sovereignty over everything in the universe includes even evil. He uses it to bring about His own will. For example, the Church seems to rejoice about original sin when it prays: "O blessed fault to merit such a Redeemer" (Easter Vigil liturgy). God's goodness wins out, hands down. In fact, there is never any question about it.

Putting all of this together, Christians know that there will be a definite resolution to life. Not only that, but they know that the resolution will be something good and desirable. To believe in the Good News that God *is* Love is to declare that life is a comedy (in the Greek sense). No matter what kinds of setbacks and difficulties the heroes (we) have to go through, we know that it all works out for the best.

Andrew Greeley says that this is the amazing realization "that the Universe is out to do you good" (Chapter 3, *The Jesus Myth*). This is what lies at the core of the meaning of the Second Coming — Good News — Love is perfected, Jesus is totally revealed. God wins, evil is destroyed.

THE DAY OF THE LORD

Hopefully, I've adequately summarized the significance of the *event* of the Second Coming. But what we've seen so far is just the beginning of the Gospel teaching on eschatology (study of the last things). As I mentioned earlier, Jesus explained His coming again *within* the Old Testament Hebraic understanding of "the day of the Lord" (parallel to Daniel 7). He did this seemingly to indicate that He is the Messiah King that the Jews were awaiting. In a similar way He quotes Isaiah, "The Spirit of the Lord is upon me. He has anointed me to preach the Good News, etc...." and adds, "This passage of scripture has come true today as you heard it being read" (Luke 4:21 — TEV) to indicate His *fulfilling* the Old Testament revelation. He does the same thing in reference to His coming in glory: He uses what were then almost stock phrases. Any educated Jew knew what He was talking about; namely, that He is the Son of Man who institutes the Kingdom.

Jesus seems to have used the then familiar apocalyptic symbolism in an indirect way — so that people would recognize who He is. In other words, the basic teaching of the end time soars far higher than fear and horror. For example, He doesn't add any specifics about what will happen ("tribulation") which are different from Daniel's picture. What He seems more concerned about is *how we should live* in light of the *fact* of His coming again.

READINESS

The conclusion to many of Jesus' parables is: "Watch out, then, because you do not know the day or hour" (Matthew 25:13 — TEV). This preparedness means first of all being faithful to the responsibilities of service in the Kingdom (e.g., the parable of the talents and the wise and unwise servants — Matthew 25:14-30). Jesus goes to great lengths to prevent us from deceiving ourselves into imagining that there won't be an accounting for what we've done. It's almost as if He's saying, "If you can't do it for love, at least do it because otherwise you'll get caught."

When I was in college we had a dorm proctor who taught us this sense of watchfulness. Besides having an inexhaustible supply of energy (he ran on three hours of sleep) and a lot of wisdom, this rare individual was also the proud possessor of an absolutely noiseless footstep and a near psychic sense of timing. Before you even started to enjoy some illegal activity, he just appeared miraculously by your side, in your room, parking lot, etc. After a while, it seemed that as soon as we started to think about doing something wrong, he would just happen to pass by as if to let us know that he'd be there if we did. After about three or four of these spoil-sport apparitions, we even gave up thinking about wrongdoing — we *knew* he'd find out. Just the possibility of his presence kept us in line. By some intuition he discovered that we were at this point. He no longer materialized: we were now trustworthy. In the same way

Jesus wants us to know that He is always there and that He might come to demand an accounting at any time. So why even bother to deceive Him? However, we must keep in mind that this is the *minimum* of dedication that Jesus requires. Most people have a pretty good grasp of this idea.

BUILDING THE KINGDOM

The second implication of this preparedness is that we have a responsibility to *work* to build the Kingdom. "When much has been given a man, much will be required of him" (Luke 12:48). One reason why many people ignore this duty is that they don't feel that they've been given very much. In the Parable of the Talents everyone is given something, no matter how little it is, and is expected to make it grow. It's the typical attitude of the one-talent man to despair: "Those other guys got a lot more. They can afford to take risks. I've got to play it safe." But there is no compromise: "Whoever tries to preserve his life will lose it; whoever loses it will keep it" (Luke 17:33).

It's common to say, "I'm just a layman; I can't do much to build the Church. The priests have the time and the education; let them do it. I have to worry about the security of my family and job. I can't take the risk of losing that."

> "I was afraid, so I went off and hid your money in the ground. Look! Here is what belongs to you." "You bad and lazy servant!" his master said. "You knew, did you, that I reap harvests where I did not plant, and gather crops where I did not scatter seed? Well, then, you should have deposited my money in the bank, and I would have received it all back with interest when I returned. Now, take the money away from him and give it to the one who has ten thousand dollars. For to everyone who has, even more will be given, and he will have more than enough; but the one who has nothing, even the little he has will be taken away from him. As for this useless servant — throw him outside in the darkness; there he will cry and gnash his teeth.
>
> (Matthew 25:25-30 — TEV)

This is the absolute statement that there is no way to legalize your way into the Kingdom. You can't coast along or "just make it." There is no "minimum requirement" except that of your whole heart, mind, soul and strength. And building the Kingdom has a much broader application than individual development. It is the overall responsibility of the people of God to work for the creation of a society of freedom and love for all men. Too often Christians preoccupied with the rewards of heaven ignore the needs of their fellow men, because "the world is passing away." It's a world of "toils and snares," and all you can do is suffer through it to get your "pie in the sky." Marx's "opium of the people" is a Christianity that preaches, "Stay where you are. Don't long for a better life. This is God's will for you. You'll be rewarded in heaven. Don't worry that those people are hungry or in prison or naked or sick. God will take care of them in the next life." Jesus countered such a warped view of the Gospel once and for all with His striking declaration: "I assure you, as often as you neglected to do it to one of these least ones, you neglected to do it to me" (Matthew 25:45). If anything, the call to live in the light of His coming is an increased responsibility to help transform the world. As the Vatican Council states:

> This Council exhorts Christians, as citizens of two cities, to strive to discharge their earthly duties conscientiously and in response to the gospel spirit. They are mistaken who, knowing that we have here no abiding city but seek one which is to come, think that they may therefore shirk their earthly responsibilities. For they are forgetting that *by the faith itself* they are more than ever obliged to measure up to these duties, each according to his proper vocation. *(The Church Today,* Art. 43)

This creates an attitude toward service to the world:

> Thus, far from thinking that works produced by man's own talent and energy are in opposition to God's power, and that the rational creature exists as a kind of rival to the Creator, Christians are convinced that the triumphs of the human race are a sign of God's greatness and the

185

flowering of His own mysterious design. For the greater man's power becomes, the farther his individual and community responsibility extends. Hence it is clear that men are not deterred by the Christian message from building up the world, or impelled to neglect the welfare of their fellows. They are, rather more stringently bound to do these very things. *(The Church Today,* Art. 34)

A KINGDOM OF SERVICE NOW

Implicit in this responsibility to build up the earth is that it is valuable in itself. God will perfect what we do now. Human truth and human beauty are not obliterated in the end; rather, they are preserved, glorified and re-established in Christ. This means that Christian hope is never a separation of "spiritual" things from merely "human" things. Unfortunately, Christians have often regarded human activity as a distraction from salvation. People who were involved in the world (housewives, workingmen, politicians) often felt that they couldn't be holy because they had too much *contact* with the things of this world.

Jesus' teaching on the Second Coming, however, plunges us into the present — to be caught up in love and service here and now. We are not to withdraw from society which isn't holy enough and to waste away, pining for the heavenly Jerusalem. If you want to see the Kingdom of Heaven, don't look to the sky — you might stumble and fall because you couldn't see your way. Look to your brother, create the Kingdom now, live the Father's will on earth as in heaven.

The Wedding Feast is all ready. Come in and celebrate now. Don't hesitate or wait to buy something or bring someone — *now* is the time to enter the Kingdom. Don't be like the foolish virgin who couldn't welcome the Bridegroom because she forgot to be prepared. Don't worry about tomorrow or about the cares of this life, or you might be too preoccupied to accept the invitation. Take hold of every opportunity to love, to re-create the world. Celebrate love now and you'll celebrate it forever.

This attitude of waiting in joyful hope is focused on the person of Jesus, not on any apocalyptic horrors or heavenly bliss. Christians are those who love His coming (2 Timothy 4:8). Should we become engrossed in the specifics of what heaven's like or how gory Armageddon is? Or should we rather focus on Jesus? We tend to think of the Second Coming as something totally alien to the rest of Christian life. Yet to love His coming is remarkably like any other aspect of Christian life; it's a call to know and love Jesus as a person. Then and only then do we want Him to come.

How should we wait for Jesus? Basically the same way we wait for anyone we love. Imagine that your beloved was away on vacation, and you didn't really know when he or she was returning. How would you live? First of all you'd want to be prepared so that "everything's right when she comes back." You wouldn't be too concerned with how she travelled as long as she got home quickly. You wouldn't be too worried if she didn't bring any present for you, although it would be a nice extra. This, then, is how we wait for Jesus — longing for our lover to come home.

A PILGRIM CHURCH

So far, I've been talking about the attitude of expectant hope in terms of our everyday, individual lives. There is also a certain attitude toward the Church which comes from the parables of the end time.

> The Kingdom of heaven is like a man who sowed good seed in his field. One night, when everyone was asleep, an enemy came and sowed weeds among the wheat, and went away. When the plants grew and the heads of grain began to form, then the weeds showed up. The man's servants came to him and said, "Sir, it was good seed you sowed in your field; where did the weeds come from?" "It was some enemy who did this," he answered. "Do you want us to go and pull up the weeds?" they asked him. "No, he answered, "because as you gather the weeds you might pull up some of the wheat along with them. Let the wheat and the weeds both grow together until harvest, and then I will tell the harvest workers: Pull up the weeds first and tie them in bundles to throw in the fire; then gather in the

wheat and put it in my barn." (Matthew 13:24-30. Explanation: 13:36-43)

The implications of these parables are that the Church is growing. In this particular parable we see the perfect description of the pilgrim Church. We are a Church of sinners growing to holiness, going somewhere. The Kingdom is not perfect — never will be until the Lord comes again. We are to expect people to have all the limitations of their sinfulness. Christians, already experiencing the love and power of God, will still fall, be insensitive, get depressed occasionally, make mistakes. There will always be phony Christians and hypocrites. Even Jesus expected that. That's life. "Accept it," the Lord says, "and don't try to force the Church to be perfect." Very often we understand how weak we can be and yet expect others (especially Church leaders) to be without fault. Throughout history, people have over and over again tried to separate themselves from worldly Christians in order to create the pure and holy remnant to be the real Church. Conclusively, it has never worked. The pure believers, in ripping out the weeds, often destroy the fruit of their own faith. In the end they too become "worldly," and a new group separates and becomes the "true Church." This process is summarized beautifully by Ronald Knox:

> The enthusiast wants to see results; he is not content to let the wheat and the weeds grow side by side until the harvest. It must be made possible somehow, even in this world, to draw a line between the sheep and the goats. Thus a little group of devout souls isolates itself from the rest of society to form a nucleus for the New Jerusalem; and in doing so, it loses touch with currents of thought that flow outside, grows partisan in its attitude, sterile of new ideas.

(Enthusiasm, p.229)

It's *not* our job to decide who's living a truly Spirit-full life. The Lord is the Judge. The Kingdom is *in* the world, with all its failings and frustrations. This is the locale of the Spirit's action. The yeast of the Spirit must be mixed with the flour of the world and mankind. Anyone knows that if you try to take the flour away, you won't get any bread. Only in the end will the Lord decide who's leavened by love and who's still not transformed. "Then God's people will shine like the sun in their Father's Kingdom. Listen, then, if you have ears!" (Matthew 24:43 — TEV)

This parable also means that human society will never be perfected by its own efforts. "Creation was made subject to futility, not of its own accord but by him who once subjected it . . ." (Romans 8:20). There will always be evil in society and evil in men. People will always reject Love and Jesus right up until the end. No new knowledge or technological breakthrough or political system or brilliant leader will be able to create a perfect society. In fact, an overall theme of apocalyptic symbolism is that there will be a gradual polarization of good and evil. Human progress is making men more free, more aware of the options of life and more able to actualize their choice. As our potential and power for good grows, so does our power for evil. Man can heal almost miraculously, but he can also kill on a truly demonic scale. The good get better and the bad get worse.

C. S. Lewis seems to think that this is the atmosphere of the book of Revelation. Mankind progresses till all people have a free choice about who they want. Ultimately it comes down to the Antichrist versus the people of God. They are in all ways at war. This is the harvest time. Men's hearts and deeds are revealed, and Jesus comes to separate and gather His own for the new creation.

WHEN WILL ALL THIS OCCUR?

A favorite question at this point is, "It sounds great that Jesus will come again, but do you have any idea *when* He will come?" A most intriguing query, and the infinity of answers to it have amazed, appalled and amused the Church since it began. Every generation has its prophecies of doom, predictions of catastrophe, secret codes and number systems, all to announce for the first time with certainty the day and hour of the Lord's coming. Along with falling in love, the generation gap and warfare, it's one of the rare streaks of consistency in our all-too-fickle race.

It's obvious that I am skeptical of the theology of the Lord's imminent coming, for reasons that are at once very scriptural and very traditional. Yet I can readily sympathize with the people who hold this attitude. For the most part, those who preach this nearness of the Second Coming really *want* Jesus to come, and that's beautiful. I too long for Jesus to come, but I don't think that He has to follow my timetable. He'll come in the "fullness of time," at the time the Father, in His wisdom, has chosen. All of my desire for Jesus' coming, no matter how sincere and faithful, will not force Him to come. He'll come when He chooses to come. After all, He's free also.

> But do not forget this one thing, my dear friends! There is no difference in the Lord's sight between one day and a thousand years; to him the two are the same. The Lord is not slow to do what he has promised, as some think. Instead, he is patient with you, because he does not want anyone to be destroyed, but wants all to turn away from their sins.
> But the Day of the Lord will come as a thief.
>
> (2 Peter 3:8-10)

Jesus may come tomorrow or in a million years. And all of my desire doesn't lessen His freedom. I think that most of the people who preach the impending Second Coming truly love God in a very special way, yet they seem to have mistaken their own desire for God's plan.

A second popular reason for expecting the Lord to come soon is the desire to have Him complete the renewal of the Church. Many have caught hold of a vision of what the Church can be. People are changed, a community of love springs up; the Spirit is certainly at work. Yet, after a while, the vision fades. People drop out, and it looks like this renewal might end up like all the other renewals: in twenty, fifty or a hundred years there'll be a "dead" Church again. So rather than risk this tragedy, we can hope that Jesus will come before the renewal dies. His coming will catch it at its highest peak and therefore save all our hard work from going down the drain. Then the renewal will be like a champion athlete dying young. It will avoid all the pain and disappointment of old age, and the challenge of middle age. Like ending a marriage after the honeymoon, Jesus will save us from the doldrums of working the Spirit into our everyday lives.

In reality, though, the Second Coming is "The Renewal" of the Church, and everything else till then is only a dim image and a promise of the fullness of what will be. Historically renewals display a tendency to die out quickly and often profess to be "the latter rain" of the Spirit (Joel 2:23) which precedes the end. Charismatic renewals or revivals are, in fact, usually characterized by the preaching of the return of Jesus (see Knox, *Enthusiasm,* chapter 8). And the moment a movement becomes "apocalyptic" is typically the instant it stops hoping for the renewal of *the present society.* Again, this seems like we're pursuing our own desires to safeguard our movements, rather than trusting God's plan "... to bring all things in the heavens and on earth into one under Christ's headship" (Ephesians 1:10). I don't want to see the present renewal pass away, but the guarantee of that is the Holy Spirit and our love. God doesn't save movements; He only saves sinners like us.

Not too surprisingly, we find these same attitudes expressed in Scripture (See I & II Thessalonians; I Corinthians 15; II Peter 3). Even the apostles, on fire from their encounters with the risen Lord, expect this sudden return:

> While they were with him they asked, "Lord, are you going to restore the rule to Israel now?" His answer was: "The exact time it is not yours to know. The Father has reserved that to himself.
>
> (Acts 1:6, 7)

The certainty and clarity of this statement cannot be misinterpreted. *It's not for you to know* — don't worry about it; don't even guess, because it's beyond your understanding. Instead, Jesus commands them to (1) be filled with the Holy Spirit, and (2) be witnesses to Him throughout the world. It's a shame that so many, attempting to know the day and the hour, lose sight of the essential task of yielding to the Spirit and proclaiming the Good News.

191

Throughout the New Testament the Lord is described as coming like a thief in the night, at an hour when we are not expecting Him (Matthew 24:43, 44). This theme is constant in the parables, as if to stress the Christian's call to expectancy and preparedness. The very fact that we don't know when the Lord will return creates in us the attitude of wide-awake living in the present. "Be sure of this: if the owner of the house knew when the thief was coming he would keep a watchful eye and not allow his house to be broken into" (Matthew 24:43). We are to live as if the bridegroom could come at any time — early or late — and to be prepared at every moment. If it's soon, we greet Him. If it's late, we work and build His Kingdom, always ready for Him. It was the foolish virgins who didn't prepare to wait for the Lord. "The groom delayed his coming," and to the ones who ran out of oil (faith, love, etc.), He said, "I do not know you" (Matthew 25:1-13). That's what happens when you try to second-guess God.

Probably the most enlightening passage on the topic is this one: "As for the exact day or hour, no one knows it, neither the angels in heaven, *nor the Son,* but the Father only" (Matthew 24:36). It's important to understand that most Scripture scholars consider this passage to be highly authoritative. That is, it almost certainly records the words of Jesus Himself. Aside from textual proofs, the main reason for their opinion is that it is inconceivable that the evangelists would have added on, as a teaching, the notion that Jesus was ignorant of anything, let alone His own Second Coming. The tradition must have been overwhelming that these were Jesus' actual words. It is also a testimony to the honesty of the Gospel authors that they would retain a phrase which would cause immense doctrinal problems then and now. Also, it seems that this passage was inconsistent with the atmosphere of the first Christian centuries. There was quite an apocalyptic fervor in the early Church, and these passages (along with Acts 1) would have gone directly against the prevailing mood. We have to conclude that if Jesus did not know, we should not even guess.

Despite all this, people have consistently claimed to be more knowledgeable than Jesus. The more spectacular errors come immediately to mind — the people who, generation after generation, expected the Lord in their own time. There is a tendency to think that all of these people were kooks and self-proclaimed prophets. Yet there were many respected and learned men who held these opinions: Nicolas of Cusa thought 1786 was the end; Erasmus, Kepler, and almost the entire Church thought that the year 1000 marked the end of the millenium mentioned in Revelation 20.

IGNORING HIS COMING

Yet a much more pervasive error is theirs who "know" that Jesus will *not* come in their time. These are the people who through fear, ignorance or laziness disregard Jesus' teaching about His coming again. They think He is a long way off, so they fall asleep on the job like the foolish virgins. They are the ones who have time to repent. They think that there will always be another day to feed the poor, help the sick, etc., but right now they have more important concerns. "I mean, a person has to provide for the future; I need security now; I have to build a career and enjoy life while I can." More and more they become entangled in the values of this life which choke off the word of God (Mark 4:18, 19). Building for a future which might never come, trapped in the mazes of their own past, they live without the joy of the present or the excitement of hope.

Now we do not know the day or the hour — whether it is near or far. But, to me, those who rationalize for a lot of time are more against the spirit of the Good News. "I know you are neither hot nor cold. How I wish you were one or the other — hot or cold! But because you are lukewarm, neither hot or cold, I will spew you out of my mouth!" (Rev. 3:15-16).

This does not mean that we jump to the conclusion that Jesus will come in 1985 or 2000. This kind of predicting, it is true, has led to zeal and dedication. More often than not, however, it has ended in sadness, division and spiritual elitism.

THE LESSONS OF HISTORY

At this point it would be helpful to look at a few examples from the early Church. We can acquire a discernment from the study of history, from being able to see the long-range fruits of any spirituality. Weeds and wheat look alike when they are young, but after a while they show their true character. The same applies to spiritual renewals. At the beginning, the Franciscans and the Waldensians had many points of similarity, yet in the long run the first was unifying and the second divisive.

Montanism was one of the more camouflaged weeds of renewal. It apparently started out as a prophetic revival which was widely recognized as authentic. Tertullian, at that time an outstanding theologian, became a Montanist because of their witness of purity and moral severity. Indeed, they were rigorists of the first degree. They considered themselves the true Church (in the Spirit, *pneumatics);* the rest of Christendom had fallen away (they were "psychic" Christians — all in the mind). I might add that this attitude and vocalulary has echoed down through the centuries and is still present in the more radical revivals. Montanism eventually developed a few more oddities: marriage was forbidden as carnal, prophecies were given in ecstatic trances, there was a possibility of payola for the more popular prophets, and eventually Montanus declared himself the Incarnation of the Holy Spirit. Finally Montanus pinpointed the time and place of the Second Coming. Trusting in the word of their prophet, the whole Montanist community trooped off to a plain in Asia Minor to await the appearance of the heavenly Jerusalem. It was going to plop into their pneumatic arms. Well, evidently the time or the location was a bit off, so they tramped back to their home town in Phrygia. And lo and behold! They discovered that their little village itself was, in truth, the New Jerusalem. And even though it might look like the same old village, those with "spiritual" eyes could discern the reality. Only pyschic (mind) Christians could fail to notice this change. Of course, every one who wanted to be "spiritual" saw the New Jerusalem. The only problem was that people continued to live in the same way, and eventually some died. Even then, Montanism took a long while to peter out; and the only thing it seemed to accomplish was to make the Church even more skeptical of the prophetic charism, especially in laymen.

A similar event occurred also in Asia Minor about the middle of the fourth century. The bishop of Antioch concluded that the Lord would come within the year. He urged the whole diocese to forsake jobs, marriages and property and to go off into the desert to fast and pray. If the Lord did not come within the year, they would never have to believe another of the bishop's words. Off flocked the docile sheep to prepare themselves. Back they came a year later. Perhaps they really did need the retreat. At least now they could ignore their slightly daft bishop.

Over and over again it has happened throughout the years, seldom with such drastic or comical results. People have prophesied, left jobs, fasted, preached, published and protested, and obviously the Lord hasn't returned. Perhaps He was expected too much.

Thus to "build . . . with . . . hay or straw" (1 Cor. 3:12) causes sadness, division and confusion — even today. Too often the spectacles of the apocalypse replace the Good News of Jesus Christ crucified, the forgiveness of sins, and the gift of the Spirit. And consistently, as soon as people are convinced of a certain date, they neglect their responsibilities of love, service and even self-sustenance to wait for the Kingdom. In Thessalonia some of the brothers refused to work because they thought the Lord's coming was just around the corner (1 Thess. 4). It seems that some people just can't resist burying their talents.

So if you walk into any Christian bookstore, you'll probably find a few books claiming to predict the demise of the late planet earth. New "secrets" will be explained, "the fulfillment of six thousand year old prophecies in our own time!" The Common Market or the World Council of Churches will be the Antichrist (to rank alongside such all-time favorites as Diocletian, Attila, Caesar, the Pope of Rome, Luther, Karl Marx, Hitler, etc.). New calculations of the end time, new tribulations, new descriptions of the rapture. Well, "What shall we say after that? If God is for us, who can be against us?" (Romans 8:31). Only the Father knows. I don't know when, how or where. Maybe the new calculations are correct. You can decide for yourself whether this is really what Jesus intended by ". . . keep

195

your eyes open, for you know not the day or hour" (Matthew 25:13). As for me, I know my Lord will come again, and that's all I need.

Finally, we can get around to how this affects our daily lives. What does the Second Coming mean for you and me? How does it change things?

THE PERSPECTIVE OF THE KINGDOM

First of all it gives us a sense of the value of history. This doesn't mean the past, as in textbooks. Rather it means the future. We have a goal. We are going somewhere, and *everything* men do can contribute to this final resolution and fulfillment in Jesus. Since Yahweh is the Lord of the nations, what men do in the secular world is also used by Him to build His Kingdom. For example, you might think it's a shame that the traditional Christian culture and values of America have broken down. Well, a more eschatological viewpoint might perceive that this seemingly bad thing frees men from an artificial "social religion" and promotes the necessity of choosing what one wants to do. Because I have options, I have to make a choice. Faith has to be more authentic now. In this, the progress of mankind in some way contributes to the building of the Kingdom.

This applies to us as individuals also. I cannot consider my human work and talent to be works of the flesh which profit nothing. My excellence in psychology, cooking, mathematics or bricklaying can be used to build the Kingdom. And not merely as a witness. The development of my creative potential helps men to be free, to be fed and sheltered, to rise eventually above themselves to love and joy.

A Christian's peace about history is rooted in God's control over it. If we recognize this, we can never despair over political chaos. The believer is called to see and live life as a comedy. Everything is going to work out in the end. Our fears of ecological, nuclear or political disaster are all overcome in the hope of God's Kingdom. We know that the earth will never be destroyed without our having a far better home. This optimism of faith is not an escape from action, but rather the reason for increased work but with less anxiety. We can never give up because we know that God will never give up on us. It's as if we were apprentices and Jesus the Master of the art of love. He has shown us how to serve and has given us a job to do, complete with tools and instructions. He wants us to become master artisans like Him; to love as He has loved us. To do that we have to work to make our own creation of love. We can't just wait around for the Master to do things: He's given us the job. It's our responsibility, yet we always know that in case of real trouble the Master will come and finish the job. This is the tension between building the earth and waiting for Jesus to sum up all creation in Himself. We can work to the fullest with the peace and relaxation of much-loved apprentices. What we do now, while good in itself, is perfected in the end.

JUDGMENT

The second basic lesson is the realization of the judgment. Nasty word, isn't it? It makes you feel as if you'll have to defend your life before an infinitely stern magistrate. Hardly something to be joyful about.

To appreciate all aspects, however, we have to understand that judgment refers not only to the Second Coming but to the present also. The word which Jesus has spoken is *now* the judgment (John 12:31), and anyone who believes in Him will not be judged, but those who reject Him have already been judged (John 3:18; 5:24). This implies that those who believe and love no longer have to fear any judgment. It also means we don't have to judge others' belief; Jesus has already done that. With this understanding, we can view the day of judgment as the moment when God validates the actions and secret thoughts of men's hearts (Matthew 25 & Romans 2:6-10). God will bring all things to light, not to pass sentence but to "reward every person according to what he has done" (Romans 2:6 — TEV). We probably won't be surprised about what happens to us. We already know whether we've lived lovingly or have rejected love. God will simply give us an eternity of what we've desired on earth, be it Himself or our own self. As a matter of fact, Jesus' very coming will indicate how we lived. If we have loved, we will not turn from Him in shame but welcome Him when He

197

comes. So if you want to find out what's in store for you, just ask yourself whether you love His coming.

Practically, this means that we no longer have to hide what we're really like, for "... no one makes a fool of God! A man will reap only what he sows" (Galatians 6:7).

> Be on guard against the yeast of the Pharisees, which is hypocrisy. There is nothing concealed that will not be revealed, nothing hidden that will not be made known. Everything you have said in the dark will be heard in the daylight; what you have whispered in locked rooms will be proclaimed from the rooftops.
>
> (Luke 12:1-3)

The positive aspect of the revelation of all things is very beautiful. Every good thing we've ever said or done in secret will also be revealed. For example, how many times have you daydreamed about a friend, just being happy because you know him or her? If you try to tell your friend, it all comes out wrong; or you're too shy to express how much joy he brings you. All this will be revealed. And we'll also find out all the times that others have thought well of us but never told us. At last we will find out what people really think of us. And there won't be any pain in this disclosure, because we'll be known and accepted in love. We will be completely one even as Jesus and the Father are one (John 17:21). And we will rejoice in the nakedness of our hearts, celebrating our sinfulness and God's forgiveness.

DIVERSE SPLENDOR UNVEILED

I often think of this oneness as a kind of universal marriage. Our union with each other will perfect us as unique individuals. In Mark Twain's heaven everyone was alike, and it was this impersonality which made it so unattractive. Yet, to be one like Jesus and the Father means that mankind is revealed in a splendor of diversity. It will be the full flowering of our personality. "Your life is hidden now with Christ in God. When Christ our life appears, then you shall appear with him in glory" (Colossians 3:3, 4).

My life changes now, in that I know that the future in Jesus is much more exciting than anything I experience. All the joy, love and wonder that I have found in life is only a dim image in a mirror (1 Cor. 13:12). I rejoice in the love and friendship that I have now, but the oneness that awaits me will be almost as if I had lived and experienced everything that every other human has experienced. It will be like living every life that could be lived. We received an insight into this reality when a young man complained about there being no marriage in heaven. A woman overheard him and immediately added, "Well, you won't need it. Can you imagine being totally married in body, mind and spirit to everyone? Who would want this one-dimensional marriage then?"

Now, I'm the kind of person who gets very frustrated when I can't really communicate my love and my deep feelings. And how feebly I understand others when they try to reveal themselves. Well, the reality of love at the Second Coming should help us to be more accepting of the weakness of the flesh now. The dream of total intimacy will be ours. Until that day we'll have to plough through headaches, misunderstandings, distrust and a degree of alienation even in the best of our relationships. And with those with whom agreement and peace seem impossible, at least we know that one day we will finally see things from their viewpoint and probably learn to laugh a lot at our own narrow-mindedness.

All of this sets me free from expecting perfection in myself and others. I am graced with acceptance because I know that perfection will come; therefore I can embrace imperfection as temporary and even necessary. For example, you don't get angry at half-baked dough if it's only been in the oven for half the time. You wait, and if the oven's still working, you know you'll get bread eventually. Well, the pilgrim Church is in a similar situation; so is the pilgrim people and each pilgrim person. We're all half-baked Christians, and the attempt to swallow one another predictably causes indigestion.

To live expecting the revealing of all things in God's judgment means many more things. Not only can we relax and start to accept ourselves as we are, but we can start to live "defenseless" lives. God is our protector and our vindicator. We are completely relieved of any need to punish or get back at someone else. We don't have to defend our reputation or our integrity. We can stop worrying about how other people think of us or what kind of status we have. Paul even suggests that we *don't even compare* ourselves with others. We are free to live for God's acceptance rather than man's approval. This also means that we can allow others the same freedom and need not expect them to live for our acceptance.

LIVING NOW IN THE NEW JERUSALEM

If you haven't guessed by now, living in the light of the Second Coming is an entirely new way of life. One area where this newness shows up very noticeably is in our attitude toward material goods.

> Do not lay up for yourselves an earthly treasure. Moths and rust corrode; thieves break in and steal. Make it your practice instead to store up heavenly treasure, which neither moths nor rust corrode nor thieves break in and steal. Remember, where your treasure is, there your heart is also.
>
> (Matthew 6:19-21)

Practically, this means that we start to value our material goods for their utility to others equally as much as for their advantage to ourselves. We *possess* nothing. Rather, we are stewards of an abundance to be distributed as the Lord sees fit. The Fathers of the Church saw this so clearly that they insisted that whatever remained beyond your own need *belonged* to the poor.

> Jews give a tenth of their goods to God; Christians give everything they have (and not just a little part) for the use of the Lord (that is to the Church for the poor), giving freely and with joy because they hope for goods of a higher order.
>
> (St. Irenaeus)

Once we start to regard the new Jerusalem as our real home,

our reality, then it follows as a matter of course that we cannot be concerned with wealth and status now. "Be on guard lest your spirits become bloated with indulgence and drunkenness and worldly cares. The great day will suddenly close in on you like a trap" (Luke 21:34; see also Luke 12:16-21).

It is important to remember that material goods are a gift for building up the Church. Like any charism and talent, they are to be used responsibly and in love. This applies to our choice of jobs as well as our money. And tremendously practical ways of sharing what we have are using our cars and opening our homes to build the community.

Another area of dramatic newness is our attitude toward personal relationships. Living in hope and expectancy involves an openness to the potential in our neighbor, whoever he is. No one is ever hopeless — not even ourselves. I don't give up on people no matter how bad off they are (or we are). This applies to our Church, our government, marriage, friendships, etc. With the Spirit and our love, the most impossible situations and people can be transformed.

Much of the reality of this hope comes from the ability to live in the present. So often we block our love simply because we are mired in the past or absorbed in the future. Just think of all the time you spend rehashing old discussions or arguments, preparing yourself for a confrontation, wasting hours in futile introspection, and mulling over endless problems. All of this leaves no room or energy for creativity and usually makes us drab. In the community we have found this mania for introspection to be a very great barrier to a person's growth in the Lord. We point out that a major part of repentance is to stop thinking of yourself. When we really take seriously Jesus' triumph in the Second Coming, we can trust in Him as the Lord of history. We can put the past behind us and trust in Him to take care of the future. This frees us to be concerned with the *now,* to be absorbed in what's presented to us and to participate in it. We have a motto on weekend retreats that fits perfectly here: "Don't anticipate." In conversations, don't anticipate what you're going to say — listen. In prayer, don't anticipate good feelings — talk to Jesus. In friendships, don't anticipate affection and understanding — communicate your needs. All of a sudden, normal life takes on the joy of being involved in the now. This is the character of play and celebration — to give your all to what's at hand.

In his book *The Second Touch,* Keith Miller tells the story about how his youngest son always used to bother him when he was reading the paper. It was always, "Look at this, Daddy! What is it?" Keith would be very irritated and would try to get rid of his son quickly so he could get back to reading. It never worked. One day someone told him to try to be completely "present" with his boy. That night when his son came up to him, he folded the paper and put it away. He always used to keep his finger in the page to hint the he was just about to start reading again. Anyway, he gave all of his attention to his son, lifted him up to his lap, gave him a hug and asked what it was that the boy wanted. To his complete surprise the child told him in thirty seconds and left. All he wanted was to be recognized and accepted, and his father's "presence" accomplished this. There was no further need to bug his father. We too can give ourselves totally to each other and to God, and we might even have more time left than we had before.

The problem is that we are told that life operates according to the work ethic. Americans, especially, are so activity-oriented that they have lost their sense of leisure, of play. "Wasting time" for love or enjoyment is no longer permissible. Contemplation is forsaken for production, and anxiety is the result. Our material good, our friendship, and even our prayer life are measured by utility. "What do you get out of it?" is the big question. Yet to wait for Jesus' coming frees us to recreate life — to give our self and our life without compromise or worry. Sister Jane Marie Richardson expresses this perfectly in an article "Joy Is the Serious Business of Heaven":

> Self is never given at a bargain, however, at least not the self that is properly valued. Yet, paradoxically, one doesn't carry on delightful exchange with God and others for any reasons of gain. We play and pray because we want to and, like to. Praying and playing stand as legitimate

expressions of human aliveness. They are good things to do in their own right and not means to an end.

When a class of first graders was asked, "Why did God make you?", one eager little fellow shot up his hand immediately. "Just for fun!", he said. Purpose is subordinate to joy.

We need not fear this "not for trade or cash" quality of play and prayer. On the contrary, living needs no justification, no apologies. One is not accountable for how he lives but how he fails to live. Time stands still in prayer and play; it is as if it were not. Far from being wasted, time fulfills itself, ushering in timelessness or life without measure. *To pray and to play means choosing life, this kind of life.*

> *(New Catholic World,* Nov./Dec., 1972, p.283)

If this sounds too frivolous, remember that Jesus described the Kingdom as a wedding banquet.

To live in hope means that we work and love now to create this future life. We can't be sidetracked by things that interfere with the wedding banquet. Why hold a grudge? The party's about to begin, so make up with your brother. Why let worry over your possessions dampen the feast? Or lust? Or hatred? "The world and everything in it that men desire is passing away; but he who does what God wants lives forever" (I John 2:17 – TEV). Love without worrying about being hurt. Give and don't consider the cost. Live as if Jesus were coming tomorrow. "Don't be worried and upset . . . I am going to prepare a place for you . . . so that you will be where I am" (John 14:1-3 – TEV).

THE RESURRECTION

Another aspect of the Second Coming which helps us to live in a new way is the resurrection of the body. We never become angels. We will always remain human beings, but our risen bodies will be incorruptible and glorious (I Cor. 15:42, 43) like Jesus', totally filled with the Spirit. "Through baptism into his death we were buried with him, so that, just as Christ was raised from the dead by the glory of the Father, we too might live a new life" (Romans 6:4). "He will give a new form to this lowly body of ours and remake it according to the pattern of his glorified body, by his power to subject everything to himself" (Philippians 3:21).

Paul considered these truths the very foundation of our faith. Jesus was raised from death and so shall we. If this is not true, then "we are the most pitiable of men" (I Cor. 15:19). "Because if the dead are not raised, then Christ was not raised; and if Christ was not raised, your faith is worthless. You are still in your sins" (I Cor. 15:16, 17).

As we grasp the import of the resurrection, through the power of the Spirit, death loses its terror. "O death, where is your sting?" (I Cor. 15:55). We can even celebrate death as the consummation of life. Death becomes the last step in a life of transformation. It is the final parting of the veil, the laying aside of the last barrier to union with Jesus.

> While we live in our present tent we groan; we are weighed down because we do not wish to be stripped naked but rather to have the heavenly dwelling envelop us, so that what is mortal may be absorbed by life. God has fashioned us for this very thing and has given us the Spirit as a pledge of it.
>
> (II Cor. 5:4, 5)

It is not that our bodies or the material world are bad; it's just that what awaits us is better. We already taste and experience the Kingdom now and in fact are being prepared for its fullness through death and the Spirit. It's a matter of degree; what we have now is good; what's in store is better. This is why we can rejoice in death.

> So we are always full of courage. We know that as long as we are at home in this body we are away from the Lord's home. For our life is a matter of faith, not of sight. We are full of courage, and would much prefer to leave our home in this body and be at home in the Lord. *More than anything else, however, we want to please him, whether in*

our home here or there. For all of us must appear before
Christ to be judged by him....

(II Cor. 5:6-10 — TEV)

And what pleases God is that we love and do His will here
and now. In this we can never despair.

This hope is not merely for individuals but for all of society
and the physical universe. God will set our whole being free,
materially and socially as well as personally, since all these
dimensions are essential to being human. "All of creation waits
with eager longing for God to reveal his sons ... there was this
hope: that creation itself would one day be set free from its
slavery to decay, and share the glorious freedom of the children
of God" (Romans 8:19-21 — TEV).

Therefore, there will also be a resurrected universe.
Materiality itself dies to live in a new way. The universe is
immersed in the Spirit of God. Every good and beautiful thing is
glorified in Jesus, transformed in the same way we are
transformed: in love, in Jesus.

> Dearly beloved,
> we are God's children now;
> what we shall later be has not yet come to light.
> We know that when it comes to light
> we shall be like him,
> for we shall see him as he is.
> Everyone who has this hope based on him
> keeps himself pure, as he is pure.

(I John 3:2, 3)

"And this hope will not leave us disappointed, because the
love of God has been poured out in our hearts through the Holy
Spirit who has been given to us" (Romans 5:5).

To live in hope is to be open to the possibilities of life and
love, assured that we are already a part of the new creation in
Jesus. Only because we experience the love and power of God in
His Spirit now can we believe in this future fulfillment. This
experience strengthens our will and enhances our ability to grow
by means of the very problems and challenges of this life.
Though we struggle with divisions, poverty, inequality and

half-baked Christians, we know that "When the perfect comes, the imperfect will pass away" (I Cor. 13:10). Then ". . . there shall be no more death or mourning, crying out or pain, for the former world has passed away" (Revelation 21:4). Only Love will remain.

I hope that I have managed to communicate some of the joy which Jesus' coming brings to me. There is so much beauty in it that we can "cheer each other up with these words" (1 Thess. 4:18 — TEV). We needn't fear anymore. I found in my own life that it was the times when I wanted the Lord to come that I was most trusting and peaceful and also the most loving. For example, once I was walking back from a Mass in which the parables of the end time were read. I was in a particularly complaining mood, and all I seemed to have in mind were the infinite unsolvable problems of our own community and the Church. I began to pray and asked the Lord to tell me what His coming meant for me in my present state. All of a sudden I started to sing: "Oh, you'd better not shout, you'd better not cry, better not pout, I'm tellin' you why, Jesus Christ is coming to town." After about five minutes of solid laughter, I was once again in a peaceful, simple trust in Jesus, and this set me free to reach out and love. This is how the Second Coming can transform us now.

The best possible summary is this beautiful section from Article 39 of the Vatican Council's *Constitution on the Church in the Modern World:*

> We do not know the time for the consummation of the earth and of humanity. Nor do we know how all things will be transformed. As deformed by sin, the shape of this world will pass away. But we are taught that God is preparing a new dwelling place and a new earth where justice will abide, and whose blessedness will answer and surpass all the longings for peace which spring up in the human heart.
>
> Then, with death overcome, the sons of God will be raised up in Christ. What was sown in weakness and corruption will be clothed with incorruptibility. While

charity and its fruits endure, all that creation which God made on man's account will be unchained from the bondage of vanity.

Therefore, while we are warned that it profits a man nothing if he gain the whole world and lose himself, the expectation of a new earth must not weaken but rather stimulate our concern for cultivating this one. For here grows the body of a new human family, a body which even now is able to give some kind of foreshadowing of the new age . . .

For after we have obeyed the Lord, and in His Spirit nurtured on earth the values of human dignity, brother-hood and freedom, and indeed all the good fruits of our nature and enterprise, we will find them again, but freed of stain, burnished and transfigured. This will be so when Christ hands over to the Father a kingdom eternal and universal: "a kingdom of truth and life, of holiness and grace, of justice, love and peace." On this earth that kingdom is already present in mystery. When the Lord returns, it will be brought into full flower.

Amen! Maranatha! Come Lord Jesus!

BIBLIOGRAPHY

RECOMMENDED READING:

Abbott, Walter M., SJ, (Editor), *The Documents of Vatican II,* The America Press, New York, New York, 1966, 794pp.

See especially chapter VII of the Dogmatic Constitution on the Church, *"The Eschatalogical Nature of the Pilgrim Church and Her Union with the Heavenly Church," as well as Article 39 of* The Church Today. *These two sections contain the basic theological insight of this chapter.* The Dogmatic Constitution on Divine Revelation *would also be relevant reading.*

Lewis, C.S., *The Great Divorce,* The Macmillan Co., New York, New York, 1946, 128pp.

This is a delightful moral fantasy about heaven and hell. It is speculation and should be read as such.

SUPPLEMENTARY READING:

McKenzie, John L., SJ, *The Power and the Wisdom,* Bruce Publishing Co., Milwaukee, 1965, 300pp.

Chapter III, "The Reign of God," gives the scriptural background and exegesis for understanding the escatalogical Kingdom.

N. B. — There are few theologically sound yet readable books on this topic. Unfortunately, there is a multitude of theologically weak books on the Second Coming, ranging from enjoyable science fiction to sheer nonsense mired in an astoundingly simplistic interpretation of the Bible. If you are more theologically inclined, you might like *A Theology of Hope* by Moltmann and *A Theology of Death* by Karl Rahner.